Living Your Life with Asperger Syndrome

How a young boy and his mother deal with the challenges and joys of being eleven, brilliant and socially absent

Karra Barber

P·C·P
Paul Chapman
Publishing

Paul Chapman Publishing
A SAGE Publications Company
1 Oliver's Yard
55 City Road
London EC1Y 1SP

SAGE Publications Inc.
2455 Teller Road
Thousand Oaks, California 91320

SAGE Publications India Pvt Ltd
B-42, Panchsheel Enclave
Post Box 4109
New Delhi 110 017

www.luckyduck.co.uk

Commissioning Editor: Barbara Maines
Editorial Team: Sarah Lynch, Mel Maines, Wendy Ogden
Designer: Jess Wright
Cover Photo: Linda Johnson

A catalogue record for this book is available from the British Library
A Library of Congress Control Number is available

ISBN10 1-4129-1960-6
ISBN13 978-1-4129-1960-9

Printed on paper from sustainable resources
Printed in Great Britain by The Cromwell Press Ltd, Trowbridge, Wiltshire

With love,
I dedicate this book to Thomas –
you are my treasure.

Contents

Acknowledgements

First I'd like to thank my editor, Barbara Maines. Your sincere interest and support on this subject propelled me to complete this book. I'm indebted to Lucky Duck and SAGE for giving me the opportunity to share Thomas' journey.

Scott, thank you for your confidence and unwavering belief in me. Thanks to my family and friends who encouraged me to write Thomas' stories and bring light to Asperger's syndrome. I am especially thankful to Brad Bunnin, Bob Huddleston, Linda Johnson and Gina Pardo. A special thank you to Dr. Tony Attwood.

Barbara Trent, thank you for more than five years of consistency and steady influence in Thomas' life at school. To Carin Garton and Thomas' elementary school teachers - thanks for helping him grow and shine. I'm grateful to Clare Ames Klein, Karen Zuniga, Kim Wolfram and Jenna Krook for your insight and respect for Thomas.

And to Marc, your generosity and wonderful spirit has enriched our lives immeasurably.

Introduction

Hans Asperger was an Austrian pediatrician. In 1944, he published his documented observations of groups of children, predominately boys, exhibiting a host of behavior patterns which included:

- lack of interest in social interaction

- lack of empathy

- intense focus on special interests

- and motor clumsiness.

Decades later, in 1981, a British researcher named Lorna Wing, published a paper which further described the intricacies of Asperger's syndrome. It wasn't until 1991 that Uta Frith translated Asperger's original paper from German to English, which largely contributed to the research defining Asperger's syndrome.

Today, research suggests that Asperger's syndrome (AS) is a neurobiological disorder on the Autistic Spectrum. In 1994, the Diagnostic Statistical Manual Fourth Edition (DSM IV) added the diagnostic criteria for AS. These distinguishing characteristics are often referenced and used for the purpose of diagnosis.

In preparing the introduction for *Living Your Best Life with Asperger's Syndrome*, I shared with my eleven year old son Thomas exactly how the name Asperger's syndrome was derived. I explained that a man named Hans Asperger was a scientist who was interested in knowing how certain children thought and interacted with others. I told him that because he was a scientist, Dr. Asperger collected information noting children who had similar behaviors and interests.

'A scientist?' Thomas interrupted. 'That's interesting.'

'Isn't it?' I knew that would get his attention. 'I think all doctors are really scientists on some level.'

'I think it's kind of a coincidence... don't you, Mom?'

'What is?' I asked.

'The fact that he was a scientist and I'm going to be a scientist; and that he was Asperger and I have Asperger's,' he said, pointing out the obvious parallel.

'It's interesting for sure!' I told him.

Chapter One

History

Car conversation

While riding along in the back seat of our car, my eleven year old son, Thomas, reads a book on Asperger's syndrome and asks, 'Mom, in this book, they talk about Asperger's Disorder. Why do they refer to Asperger's as a disorder?'

'Not sure, but it's a good question,' I tell him.

He continues, 'I'm going to write the author of this book and tell her she used an incorrect term. Actually, I'm not in disorder. I am definitely in-order.'

'Great idea,' I reply.

A decade ago, Asperger's syndrome was a term unfamiliar to many in society. Today, evidence suggests that the prevalence rate has dramatically increased and over time, due to the pervasiveness of diagnosed cases and the rise in media attention, the general public will become more aware of the social anomalies associated with AS.

In the beginning...

I clearly remember driving home from the hospital the day Thomas was born. It was about 9:00pm and the sky was very dark. I rode home next to him while he slept snuggled in his car seat. Suddenly Thomas began to scream; no, actually wail. What on earth could be wrong? He'd been sound asleep. I quickly pushed back the top part of the car seat so I could see his face. Evidently, his new born baby cap had pushed its way down past his eyes so that he couldn't see or open his eyes (not that he was awake). I gently moved the cap back up to his forehead and told him he was okay. He immediately stopped crying. He looked into my eyes and caught my stare. I acknowledged to him why I thought he was upset and held his little fingers in my hand. He fell quietly back to sleep. In retrospect, I find it to be very telling of how he responded to the pressure and/or stimuli back then. Sensory issues became more noticeable as Thomas developed.

His behavior as a baby was fairly typical for the first year of his life. He was a good baby and never really cried unless he was tired, hurt or hungry; and even those cries were brief. He was generally very easy to please and had very few demands. He often seemed curious about how things worked, and would focus on objects that fit together and came apart. Still, he wasn't communicating well and spent a lot of 'alone time' lost in thought. He would wander around the room sometimes appearing aimless, until something caught his attention. If he found a book that held his interest he could sit for thirty minutes at a time and examine each page.

'Something is a little different,' was my mantra for the first few years of Thomas' life.

He turned one, then two, then three years old and although he seemed very bright and understood everything I said to him, he really didn't speak much. In fact, much of what he did say was unintelligible. He would communicate with me nonverbally, pointing and gesturing in response to my questions. He knew his shapes, colors and numbers. I discovered he could write his own name before his third birthday. He loved books, so I read to him often – hoping to encourage his speech and language. Later, I would learn that he had taught himself to read... brilliant!

Still, he didn't speak much

When I took Thomas to his pediatrician for his regular check ups, I repeatedly pointed out his obvious lack of speech to his doctor. The response was always the same. He reassured me that 'boys are slower' or 'this is your first child' or 'he appears alert and cognitive.' Still, when I observed him around other children his age, there were noticeable differences. I wasn't neurotic. I was a mother who chose not to ignore something that everyone else was afraid to admit. Something was definitely wrong. He was different!

Several doctors later, at age two and a half, Thomas was diagnosed with 'a speech and language deficit'. That's what they called it. He immediately began receiving speech therapy three times a week in sixty minute sessions. Over six months, Thomas made little progress and other obstacles became evident. Rigidness, sensory overload and social behavior were growing issues. The demand for even more structure and predictability became necessary. Thomas was trapped inside a brain limited by language, rigidness and sensory input. He didn't communicate much and I didn't know how to reach him. These disconnects created confusion that was manifested in his behavior.

'He's fine. He's good. Boys are slower. Don't worry.' I heard this over and over again. Family members, friends and doctors tried to assure me that Thomas was a 'normal' toddler. Perhaps it was the frequent visits to the neighborhood park that made me realise he was different. I started to observe other children of all ages running around laughing, playing and interacting with each other, while Thomas sat alone in the sand. While he enjoyed playing at the park surrounded by other children, he really preferred to play by himself. I realised he seemed uncoordinated when he walked, ran, or climbed up the stairs of the play structure. He was different.

I saw that loud noise, certain clothing and getting his haircut were extremely problematic for him. I also noticed that while he had a great appetite, he was a picky eater. He seemed to avoid certain food textures in his mouth and on his hands. Despite all these signs there was the glaring fact that I could not ignore – he wasn't speaking much. When he wanted something, he jargoned in a way that only made sense to him. Finally, he would point, I would guess, and we would move on from there. Eventually I would come to know what he wanted; either that or he simply gave up.

At the age of three, Thomas was given the broader diagnosis of Pervasive Developmental Disorder (PDD), an Autistic Spectrum Disorder (ASD). Uttering very few words at that point, Thomas worked closely with two Speech and Language therapists: Mrs Leanne, from Easter Seals and Ms Karen from the California Hawaii Elks Program. Mrs Leanne assessed Thomas' abilities and created a plan to increase his language skills. She worked with Ms Karen to assist in implementing a multi-dimensional speech and language program developed specifically for Thomas.

Initially, Ms Karen was hesitant to take on another client, as she had a very full client list. Fortunately, on the day she came to visit Thomas, he was happy and receptive. The minute she introduced herself to him, he clumsily hugged her and then plopped himself right into her lap. He'd never done that to a stranger before. I distinctly remember her looking up at me and telling me she would absolutely find a way to fit him into her schedule. There was definitely a connection!

Ms Karen knew sign language and incorporated it with the Picture Exchange Communication System (PECS), in order to encourage Thomas to communicate. She taught Thomas how to sign a few words such as more, mine, Mom, out, no, help, yes etc. I remember being concerned that if Thomas learned sign language he might then rely on that form of communication and never attempt to communicate verbally. Ms Karen assured me that in all her years as an SLP that had never happened. As part of the PECS program, Ms Karen had me take photographs of Thomas' favorite things. I took pictures of his favorite toys, trains, books, videos, clothes and blanket. I also took photographs of every room in our house, including the yard and neighborhood park. I even snapped shots of his breakfast, lunch, dinner and snack foods. From there we created a schedule for Thomas using the pictures. They were arranged in order according to his routine and placed that way on the refrigerator. The hope was that Thomas would point to one of the pictures in order to communicate his needs. It worked.

Within several months Thomas began to communicate. Both Ms Karen and Mrs Leanne continued to visit Thomas at our home on a weekly basis over the next year. Interestingly, whenever Ms Karen spoke to Thomas verbally she would also sign to him the same sentence. The assumption was that, if given two modes of communication, he would pick up one or both in an effort to communicate. And he did. Actually, he used three. Thomas began using several words, a number of signs and incorporated PECS. Eventually, the signing and PECS fell away as his language skills continued to improve.

Different sensory experiences

Sensory issues became more noticeable as Thomas developed. Although he had a healthy appetite and was receptive when introduced to pureed foods, he became less eager to eat when introduced to solid foods. When he was about two, this became an area of great concern to me. At that time, he only ate about five different things: milk, yoghurt, pretzels, bread sticks (only from the local pizza shack) and Cheerios. He had a breakdown if anything else was even introduced. I spoke to his doctor about the nutritional aspect and discussed options for other alternatives. I explained to him that it wasn't just that Thomas had a preference for specific foods, it was that he strongly avoided certain textures. Thomas had such an aversion that I knew something was different. This was not typical.

About the same time, I noticed that Thomas had a similar avoidance to wet or thick textures on his hands. Play-Doh, glue, or paint, for example, would send him right into a meltdown. In his preschool program, all of those products were used regularly for art and craft projects. Although Thomas really enjoyed art, he had to work extremely hard to overcome his issue with textures. He was really interested in the creative activities and eventually, with a lot of work, he desensitised himself from touching Play-Doh and paint. Damp paper towels were always placed right next him. He never did get over the sticky glue thing.

There were special interests too. Surprisingly, Thomas became absolutely fascinated with Play-Doh and would build elaborate miniature snowmen (always snowmen) with incredible detail. He was, and still is, extraordinarily artistic. He draws and paints exceptionally well. He's since become a master of Play-Doh creations and clay sculpturing.

Next he became focused on a small plastic watering can. He carried it everywhere he went, although he never watered any plants or flowers. Later his attention switched to trains. First he was taken with a tiny blue, Little Engine That Could toy train. Subsequent to that, it was Thomas The Tank Engine. He eventually acquired the entire train collection. In fact, when Thomas finally did learn to speak, he spoke using sophisticated language with a British dialect, as portrayed by the train characters on the Thomas The Tank Engine videos.

Eventually, Thomas came to connect words using 'borrowed text'. When he was five, he spoke in brief sentences, borrowing lines from numerous sources. Amazing! The language he used was from various conversations, books, magazines, videos and comic strips. I was impressed with his ability to take specific sentences and place them strategically into conversations that he thought were appropriate. Routinely, I would ask him from where he had borrowed these sentences and surprisingly he could accurately cite his source. I told him I thought he had an incredible skill and I encouraged him to continue. In fact, it became a game. We would practice this phrase fitting game often, and he worked diligently at placing the right phrase with an appropriate social situation. Interestingly, Thomas learned to understand what fit and what didn't. I was thrilled that he was finally talking!

Once Thomas and I were riding along in the car and he asked me if we could stop at a toy store to buy him a toy. I told him, 'No, we can't stop and buy anything we want anytime we want to.' I went on to tell him about how people needed to earn money, then save money, to then spend money… blah, blah, blah.

Thomas interrupted me and said, 'You know Mom, there are some things money can't buy…' to which I quickly replied, 'That's right honey. Things like love, friendship or happiness.' All the while I was thinking – what an abstract concept, Thomas is such a concrete thinker, he's so profound, he's so deep, I am so proud. Then Thomas continued with, 'Like I was saying Mom, there are some things money can't buy, but for everything else, there's MasterCard.' 'Oh! Of course,' I said.

Still noticing the difference…

Although I knew textures, fabrics and loud sounds were problematic for him, nothing prepared me for his reaction to getting his hair cut. When he was a baby I would cut Thomas' hair and finger nails with some resistance. When he got to be older it became nearly impossible, as he informed me that he had nerve endings on the tips of his hair strands. He would refuse to allow anyone to cut his hair. When he was about three, a good friend of mine used to cut his hair while he sat in my lap and screamed. This was such an ordeal for both of us. One day, in the middle of an out of control haircut, the owner of the salon walked over to Thomas and me and abruptly asked us to leave and never to return. She said we were disrupting the entire salon full of customers and she couldn't handle the screaming. I couldn't blame her.

I tried the expensive kid friendly shops, including those that showed videos, offered candy and prizes and had chairs that were shaped like zoo animals. I even attempted salons that specialised in cutting hair for difficult tots. Thomas was so uncomfortable with the idea of getting his hair cut that it became clear that I had only one choice. I would have to resort to trimming his hair, without his knowledge, while he slept. This was challenging and complicated. I found myself waiting until the night before a family portrait or picture day at school. Occasionally, he would awake indignant and accuse me of cutting his hair. For three years, his hair was never the same length on either side of his face.

Though I'd bought him a book called Why Haircuts Don't Hurt, which he'd read in its entirety, he was still adamant that his hair did in fact have nerve endings. Over time, I've come to understand his sensory issues. Put simply, it feels different to him. Years later – though he still claims to have nerve endings on the tips of each hair strand, as a compromise, he allows me to cut his hair once a month for five minutes and he times me. He sits quietly, I cut quickly, and that's our deal.

Many children along the spectrum often have a degree of tactile defensiveness in the same regard. After researching this matter further, I discovered a book by Dr. Jean Ayers, an Occupational Therapist. She was the first who spoke about Sensory Integration and the child. According to her research, she's determined that tactile defensiveness is a sensory integrative dysfunction in which tactile sensations are overly sensitive to stimuli. She indicated in her research specifically that, 'Many tactilely defensive children cannot tolerate having their hair washed or cut. The tactile system serving the head and face is anatomically different from the system for the rest of the body, and so the defensiveness around the head may be more severe than the rest of the body.'

Children with neurological disorders, Asperger's included, often have difficulty with sensory processing, auditory processing, motor control-planning and visual perception. This has also been true for Thomas. In fact, at age four, physical therapy (PT) was added to Thomas' list of services. The Wilbarger Technique, also known as the brushing technique, was added to his program. The idea was to allow sensory input to register through effective therapy. Occupational Therapists or Physical Therapists usually facilitate this type of program. This technique was referred to as the sensory diet. It consisted of brushing the arms, legs and back with a fine brush (it was actually a surgical brush) in a downward motion with firm pressure, for about five minutes. Next, joint compressions were added to the mix. This involved actually pushing together the joints of the major extremities, ten times each joint. The last phase included swinging back and forth for ten minutes. This was modeled and observed by the Occupational Therapist for accuracy. In conjunction with this program, a standard occupational therapy (OT) plan was incorporated for Thomas. This was to address the combination of auditory, visual and motor limitations due to his Sensory Integration Dysfunction (SID).

Thomas loved to draw. When he was five, I enrolled him in the local community arts program. Their classes were small, controlled and the social setting was quiet. This calm environment was perfect for him. It was also a good opportunity for him to interact with his peers about a shared interest. Thomas enjoyed working with clay and has since developed quite a talent. Claymation art was one of his many talents recognised by his peers.

A year later, Thomas and I were at a local park when a woman walked up to him and asked if he'd recognised her from the summer art program. Apparently, she was one of the assistants and vividly remembered Thomas. In fact, she told him she'd kept one of his train paintings because it was so incredible. 'You were a remarkable young artist, Thomas. I hope you're still enjoying art,' she said to him. As she walked away, Thomas beamed with pride.

The local community center offered many programs for the arts. An Art-Drama combination class was another one Thomas enjoyed. When he was about seven, I signed him up for a drama class with his peers. He'd frequently act out parts of stories he'd read, mimicking voices as well. Fortunately for Thomas, his teacher was fun, creative and engaging. Her name was Christine, and she and Thomas became fast friends. Alli, also a student in the drama class, was quite fond of Thomas. She'd remembered him from when they were in Kindergarten together.

On the day of one of their first performances, an audience of proud parents filled the auditorium, clapping each time a child paraded their colorful costume and decorative hat. Every child had an opportunity to read a brief description about the costume they'd made. When it was Thomas' turn, Alli felt a compelling need to encourage him. When Thomas started to speak she immediately rushed over towards him – squeezing herself by her fellow classmates, shouting in a loud whisper, 'You can do this, Thomas. Good job, Thomas...you're doing great.' She was extremely genuine and the audience thought it was quite sweet, but Thomas didn't. He was bothered by the interruption and awkwardly began again. This time, still trying to be helpful, Alli stood by his side. Then she leaned over his shoulder and began mouthing the words along with him. Again, the audience laughed. Without looking at her – Thomas stopped short and abruptly reached up and handed her his paper shouting, 'Here, you read it.' Alli stood frozen while Thomas walked back to his seat. The audience cheered and clapped.

Later I explained to Thomas that Alli was sincerely trying to be helpful but that I completely understood his frustration. After he'd calmed down, we role-played some phrases he could say next time should he find him self in a similar situation.

The following summer Thomas signed up for Robot Camp. He, along with ten other neurotypical peers, spent one week building a robot car for three hours a day. Thomas loved robots! Although Thomas had an assistant in the classroom, the teacher had difficulty with Thomas. The day before he was to finish his robot model, I received a telephone call from the teacher saying he would be unable to complete the camp. He told me I could have the unfinished robot parts for him finish at home. He explained that Thomas got upset with another student and tried to wreck their completed robot when they wouldn't let him hold it. Thomas confirmed the story. Although I understood that Thomas' frustration or unpredictable behavior was an issue for the teacher, and perhaps the students, I felt Thomas was entitled to complete the class. He'd put four days into building his robot, not to mention my $150 fee for the class. As a compromise, I offered to attend the last day of camp with Thomas so he could finish. He did, and he's never played with the robot since.

Still addressing sensory issues...

When Thomas was six and a half he tried out for T-Ball with his neurotypical peers. I thought the hand to eye coordination practice would improve his motor skills. His team was called the Mets. He always played an outfield position – but never kept track of where the ball was. His coach was a woman and on game day, she'd lay out 'carpet squares' for her players to sit on while they waited to bat. Though she was patient and enthusiastic with all her players, she was especially supportive of Thomas when it was his turn up to bat. He required additional coaching, as he only ran around the bases – if and when it occurred to him! I don't think he clearly understood the rules of the game, nor did he care. Though he held out until the end of that season, he informed me that he didn't want to play T-ball anymore, ever. 'Not only does the pollen affect my allergies, it's the most boring game on the planet. You just stand around waiting most of the game,' he explained.

Being a glutton for punishment, the next season I signed him up to be a Timber-Wolf basketball player. The games were held in an upscale school gymnasium, so a fancy (and deafening) electronic score board kept track of the games. Two basketball games were always held at the same time, and between the booming blast of the buzzer and the sound of echoing chatter, Thomas convinced me (even though he wore ear plugs) it wasn't going to work for him. 'It startles me, and it's too loud!' Strike two… Swimming, on the other hand, was a home run. Thomas found his place in the water as a Barracuda. This was a skill building swim team and was not competitive. Perfect.

Earlier on, Thomas was captivated by trains, books, dinosaurs, Play-Doh, prehistoric dragons and Lego models. Next he became passionate about sea life, art, Bionicles, Transformers and the solar system. Later his interests shifted to include things like Spiderman, Pokémon, and the Yu-Gi-Oh trading card game. Eventually he discovered ceramics, line drawing, videography, computers and script writing. 'It's my whole life,' he'd say. According to him, script writing was a skill he'd pretty much mastered and was definitely a special interest he was proud of.

Over time, Thomas' social differences and developmental history were documented. And although the early diagnosis was Pervasive Developmental Disorder (PDD), by age six Thomas was assessed again. It was determined that his characteristics were more consistent with a diagnosis of Asperger's syndrome, also an Autistic Spectrum Disorder.

Chapter Two

Grade School

Toddler

When Thomas started saying words, I was ecstatic. His first words were no, bye, dog and oh. I'd been anxiously waiting to hear him say Mom, but many months went by before he actually referred to me at all. When he did finally reference me by name, he called me Duckey. I can't explain it. There was no rhyme or reason; I just accepted the name he'd chosen for me and answered to Duckey for several years. Curiously, when Thomas was seven, my sister had her first child and I explained to him that she was a 'new mother'. That's when he immediately started calling me Mom. The reason: he wanted everyone to be clear about who belonged to which mom.

Preschool

By age four, I'd enrolled Thomas in two very different preschool prograMs One was a part time Special Education Local Plan Area (SELPA) program. There were about six English speaking children and six Spanish speaking children with varying needs. There were two special education teachers – one was bilingual – and two educational aides in that class. Several months into that program, Thomas' teacher told me that she'd heard Thomas speaking a few Spanish phrases to a couple of the Spanish speaking kids in the class. When I asked how that was possible, as he barely spoke English, she laughingly said apparently he'd identified which children only spoke Spanish and was repeating what was said to them by the teacher. Interesting. Thomas mimicked other behaviors too. Once he came home from school walking with a limp. When I spoke to the teacher about it, wondering if he'd gotten injured at school, I discovered he was modeling another child in his class who had Cerebral Palsy.

The other preschool was a typical co-op program. It wasn't long into that program before I observed Thomas wandering the room during the structured activities, while most of his neurotypical peers were able to focus. He had difficulty paying attention and Circle Time was a real struggle for him. I'd joined the co-op so that I could participate in the program with him and save financially. In retrospect, it was another opportunity for me to see his social differences in a group. I observed some of the other children and how they interacted with each other and their teacher. The disparity was obvious; Thomas behaved differently. He seemed to care less about the activity of the day unless it happened to be about trains or art. During outside time, his preference was to be alone or on a tire swing. Even when he was approached, he didn't really acknowledge the other children unless he wanted something they had. I also discovered that his gross motor skills weren't as advanced as those of his peers.

In the SELPA program, I felt Thomas was accommodated but was not particularly advancing. In comparison, his co-op preschool teachers didn't quite understand how he thought or interacted. They'd say, 'Thomas doesn't seem to view the world the same as anyone else.' He acts different because he is different, I'd remind them. In spite of their lack of understanding, I felt that a setting with neurotypical peers was a better atmosphere for him to develop and learn. He was a child that learned by example and modeled the behaviors he was exposed to such as the SELPA experience. But I also knew that for him to be successful in that environment, they would need to foster his independence in areas where he naturally excelled. Although his co-op preschool teachers didn't really identify with Thomas, they taught, protected and guided him to the best of their ability.

Kindergarten would be different. They'd know how to teach him, I thought.

Kindergarten

When Thomas entered kindergarten everything changed. Although his diagnosis at that time was Pervasive Developmental Disorder (PDD), I was confident he would excel in a general education classroom of his peers. And, in an effort to put everything on the table and share my knowledge about how to best assist him in his new environment, I collected the basic PDD literature and prepared to distribute it. I copied Thomas' assessments and evaluations pertaining to his diagnosis, along with his preschool records. I added some pertinent personal information about him from my experience. I wanted to share with them how he processed information and interacted with others.

My intention, of course, was to be accommodating and to prepare them and him for a smooth transition. I was excited. He was excited. On Registration day, Thomas and I went to the school to see who his assigned kindergarten teacher was, as well as the location of his new classroom. I didn't know anything about the teachers at that school, nor did I know enough to inquire. I guess I assumed that it wouldn't matter as long as they were informed about who Thomas was and how he learned.

After Thomas was registered we went straight to the office. I met the principal and I immediately introduced her to Thomas. He shared with her his excitement about the upcoming year while I handed her my complete and well-organised packet of information. Apparently she had already been briefed from school officials from the SELPA program, where Thomas had attended preschool. She smiled, briefly glanced at the packet and then commented to me that she hoped it would work out for us. What did that mean, I thought? Perhaps she was distracted or overwhelmed by the business of day. I chose to ignore it but definitely filed it in the back of my mind.

September 7, 1999, was the first day of kindergarten. Thomas got up in the morning, ate breakfast and got ready for his big first day of school. I took his picture as he walked out the front door. He was excited to get going so he could meet his new teacher and see his new classroom. When we arrived at the school, he immediately stood outside his classroom door and waited until the bell rang. All at once, all the children in his class quickly lined up behind Thomas, while their teacher opened her door and introduced herself to the crowd of parents and children. The teacher waited a moment, then announced to the parents that it was time to say goodbye to their children. Then she firmly requested to the children to form a straight and quiet line. She purposely waited several moments longer until parents actually hushed their children and positioned them into a place in line. It was clear that the teacher was not going to lead her group of children into her classroom, until there was complete silence and a perfectly straight line. (This should have been my first clue). Finally, while holding Thomas' hand, she led a line of quiet Kindergartners into their new classroom.

After the first week of school, the principal called a meeting. The meeting consisted of the teacher, the principal and me. As they sat around a table and cataloged Thomas' deficits, the principal suggested to me that Thomas might be better served in a different, perhaps more 'confined', environment. Justification for this was the observation that he had poor communication skills and that he didn't respond quickly to her commands. (Yes, she actually said commands). The principal was quick to offer alternative educational options for Thomas.

During the meeting, I interrupted the principal and asked her if she had reviewed the material on PDD that I had given her on registration day. It was evident to me that if she had, she might have understood Thomas and his diagnosis. Even then, never once did she ask me about PDD, what it was or how it might affect Thomas' ability to learn academically or socially. She never enquired about strategies or how either one of them might better assist him in his current classroom situation. The solution, it appeared, was simply to offer him a different placement. One idea presented to me was a Severely Handicapped (SH) class. The principal suggested that an SH class could provide Thomas with more personal attention. When I pointed out to both of them that Thomas wasn't severely handicapped, they were silent. In an earlier assessment it had been clearly documented that Thomas had absolutely no cognitive delays. However, that fact seemed to have eluded them.

I suggested that although he did require speech therapy, as he had a significant language delay and was already receiving speech and language therapy, he might benefit from some additional classroom assistance. I suggested an aide, stating I thought he would be better served in a typical classroom with his peers. In response, I was told that the teacher was having a difficult time with Thomas in her classroom, referring to how he would often walk around aimlessly when she gave directions, and said how he didn't seem to listen like the other children. She perceived him as having behavioral issues and considered him to be 'unruly'. Again, I offered the idea of an aide in the classroom.

My ideas were disregarded and seemingly I was given no further consideration. I felt that the principal had dismissed my suggestions completely and so I decided to consult directly with the school district. I immediately sent a letter to them and specifically expressed my concerns and in a follow-up telephone call I also enquired about their understanding of the situation. I was told that the 'placement' would be discussed in an Individual Education Program (IEP).

An IEP meeting was quickly scheduled. This was a team of the educators that were involved with Thomas and myself. I came to understand that the school had a very different view regarding Thomas' needs. They had a different scope because they perhaps had a different agenda. Initially, I naively believed that the school district and I would have Thomas' best educational interest as a priority. And, maybe, they thought they had. Unfortunately, the principal made the mistake of remarking to me in our initial meeting that she didn't think Thomas would fit in as a student at her school because he was different.

The IEP was to be held within the next thirty days. I realised I might be alone in thinking that Thomas would be better served in a general education classroom amongst his peers. But that was OK. In fact, it motivated me to educate myself on the Special Education Law and the rights of my son. I searched the internet and bought books on Special Education Rights and Responsibilities. I contacted state agencies that advocated and protected the rights of children under the American Disabilities Act (ADA). I researched the rights outlined in the Individuals with Disabilities Education Act (IDEA), and I learned about the legal rights and accommodations provided under the 504 Plan. I made sure I understood the importance of a Free and Appropriate Public Education (FAPE) under the law, and in the least restrictive environment. I studied and surrounded myself with resources, and networked to assist me in getting my son what I thought was necessary and appropriate for him to learn. I had become well versed in special education law and was fairly comfortable expressing my concerns regarding his needs and rights. Although I was not an expert, I felt confidently familiar with what Thomas was entitled to under the law.

The IEP consisted of a number of district personnel, Thomas' school psychologist, his current teacher, the principal and me. My role in that meeting was to advocate for Thomas and his educational needs. I knew that I would either be viewed as a great asset or a tough challenge. Either way, I would be doing my best to provide Thomas with an opportunity to be permitted to learn in a general educational setting.

In the meeting, the district gave their opinion and I responded in kind by reciting special education law (chapter and verse) under the least restrictive environment. I spoke at length about a more inclusive setting that provided educational support focusing on Thomas' academic and social needs. They presented program options, while I offered ideas and referenced inclusion models that had been successful in other prograMs After three hours of discussion, we agreed to further assess Thomas to determine more specific areas of need.

The final results included added services to Thomas' current IEP. He remained in the general education kindergarten and immediately received an increase in service hours for occupational therapy and speech and language therapy. In addition, Thomas was given full time support from a one on one educational aide. Her name was Mrs Trent.

Mrs Trent had applied for the position of an educational aide the same week that our school district posted the job description. I'm not sure if it was luck or fate, but to this day when other parents ask me how Thomas 'got' someone as wonderful as Mrs Trent, I tell them it was just meant to be! Until she'd worked with Thomas, Mrs Trent was a stay at home mother of two. She'd been out of the work force for a number of years and had never before worked as an educational aide. She was a kind and patient woman. And when she met Thomas for the first time, she seemed to have an immediate connection with him. My first impression was that Mrs Trent understood the way Thomas thought and communicated. I can't explain why.

Although Mrs Trent had limited training in the area of ASD, she was interested in educating herself and wanted to learn as much as she could about Thomas. She took several courses offered by the school district regarding special education and autism. She read folders stuffed full of literature that I'd give to her on a regular basis. We met occasionally to discuss Thomas and any pressing issues he had in the classroom. She documented his progress and noted his difficulties in a daily communication log. From time to time, Mrs Trent offered her weekends to attend conferences with me on Asperger's syndrome. She is an extraordinary person and Thomas was fortunate to 'get' her as his educational aide.

Note: About a month following that first IEP, I ran into the school psychologist at an autism conference. He had taken a 'personal day' in order to attend the conference. He told me that he was trying to educate himself further in the area of autism.

The 'Get It Factor'

Following Thomas' very difficult kindergarten year, I made it my mission to surround him with people who understood him. My idea was to build a solid foundation where he could be successful despite his learning difference. I looked for educators with personalities who would 'get it' and who would encourage him to grow and learn to the best of his ability. The 'Get It Factor' is a phrase I coined and a philosophy I follow. It has helped me to effectively identify those who could enhance Thomas' social and academic skills. This was important in an environment that was not often designed or equipped to serve him or other children who are along the autistic spectrum.

There are four levels of the 'Get It Factor':

Level one – These are the people who instinctively understand your child. They automatically know how to assist him appropriately and effectively. They know when to offer alternatives, modifications, accommodations and when to support your child. These are people who just 'get it'. Keep them on your team forevermore. In Thomas' life, they include his educational aide, his childcare provider, several teachers, some family members, grandparents and several friends and peers.

Level two – These are people who don't 'get it', but genuinely want to 'get it'. They are open-minded people who truly want to learn more so that they can understand and assist your child. These are positive people who are interested in your child's wellbeing and will eventually 'get it'.

Level Tthree – These are people who don't 'get it', but don't know they don't 'get it'. They are harmless but usually not that helpful. It's not their fault. Generally, these are people who have had limited exposure to children with Autistic Spectrum Disorders and therefore don't have the experience yet. They're sincere people who usually try to identify with your child on some level.

Level four – These are people who think they 'get it' but actually have no idea. Unfortunately they don't 'get it' at all and probably never will. In fact, they often misunderstand your child and have a tendency to complicate issues for him. They may advise you to take steps resulting in circumstances that prove to be ill-suited for your child. It's not their fault either; these people truly think they can help. They may even think they can change your child to fit in with others (square peg/round hole syndrome). They just don't 'get it'.

Thomas had always been mainstreamed with support and for him the most suitable educational environment was facilitated by a collaborative support system (people who got it) that promoted learning alternatives, opportunities, and structure. Although children with AS typically perceive the world differently, I knew Thomas would be able to achieve success if given the opportunity to unveil his real potential. That was essential.

Example of not getting it so much…

In third grade, Thomas had a substitute aide for the day. Unfortunately, substitutes don't have the luxury of being trained appropriately and apparently, she hadn't been briefed about Thomas, AS, or her role as an aide in the classroom that day. She'd arrived giving him no assistance or direction and, in fact, she expected nothing of him. Instead she insisted on doing everything for him. At some point during the day she attempted to get his attention for some reason, but when he didn't respond to her, she turned to a group of his peers at an adjoining table and said, 'Thomas doesn't pay attention. Even though I know there's something wrong with him, he's still driving me nuts!'

Thomas' peers, who thought Thomas was very smart, expressed their concern and attempted to tell the teacher. Evidently the teacher was preoccupied and therefore didn't react to the situation. The children recognised this and one boy was so bothered that after school that day he told his parents what had happened. The boy's mother called me right away. I was concerned because I knew the aide was scheduled to return the following day. When I'd asked Thomas if he'd been uncomfortable with the substitute aide and how she'd treated him, he told me she'd been impatient with him and that he would have preferred his original aide. I contacted the teacher, who felt terrible, and followed up with a complaint to the principal and school district. As a result, the aide didn't return. In this instance Thomas' peers got it even when others did not.

First Grade

Going into first grade was exciting for Thomas, but nerve racking for me. Because I felt kindergarten was such a disaster for him, I desperately wanted him to have a good experience in first grade. Fortunately, I'd heard about Mrs G and her experience in working with special students. She got it and I was grateful that she would be Thomas' first grade teacher. She had years of experience working with children who had learning differences and was known for developing a number of programs in her classroom. In fact, she was the first elementary school teacher to create a motor planning program, focusing on vestibular development. Mrs Trent was able to observe first hand how to interact with Thomas effectively by watching Mrs G, who'd specifically worked with children with Asperger's syndrome. She also demonstrated for Mrs Trent the importance of having a daily schedule for Thomas to follow. Mrs G intuitively knew the way Thomas perceived the world and how to best assist him. Each day, she created a daily routine that was written out clearly on the blackboard, knowing that predictability was a necessity for Thomas' success in the classroom. She never limited herself to traditional methods of teaching. She set the bar.

Summer school following First Grade

I thought Thomas would benefit from the school district's extended year program, so I enrolled him in the half day class that was offered in the summer time. He and Mrs Trent spent five weeks at a neighbouring school, where he continued his speech and occupational therapy per his IEP. At the time, I, along with the rest of the IEP team, felt that the consistency of his school routine should be maintained to prevent regression. Although the teacher, classroom and students were new to Thomas, the program benefited him in terms of structure and review.

One day, Thomas' summer school class took a trip to the library. The librarian had just returned from her vacation in Egypt. Excitedly, twenty first graders crowded around her while she vividly described the exotic statues and ancient pyramids she'd witnessed on her trip. Spilling facts, she pointed out where

Egypt was located on the globe. She was identifying the seven continents when Thomas eagerly raised his hand.

'Excuse me, but you do realise that the entire area [pointing to her globe] was known as Pangaea before it was separated into individual continents, right?' he announced to the librarian.

'You're absolutely right!' the librarian said, smiling, surprised by his knowledge.

Walking back to the classroom, Mrs Trent asked Thomas, 'When did you become such an expert about the continents?'

'I guess it was last year when I got a globe for my birthday,' he told her.

Note: Children who are eligible for extended year programmes can often receive just special education services without attending summer school, if academically they don't require the assistance.

Second Grade

Thomas' second grade teacher was the sweetest teacher on the planet. Her name was Mrs W. I'd heard through the grapevine that she'd known about Thomas and although she was not familiar with Asperger's syndrome, she was a teacher who was interested and receptive and felt comfortable working with Thomas. Mrs W relied heavily on Mrs Trent, intently observing how she interacted with Thomas. She and Mrs Trent decided early on that their collaboration would be necessary to educate Thomas in her classroom.

In the beginning Mrs W was gracious enough to allow me to come into her classroom and give a presentation about *The Sixth Sense*, explaining how other people perceived the world around them. *The Sixth Sense* (intuition), with regard to autism, was created by author Carol Gray. The idea was to discuss the five senses – touch, taste, smell, sight and hearing – which people used instinctively as ways to perceive information. I borrowed her information about *The Sixth Sense*, while adding games and examples to further describe how most people used their sixth sense everyday without even knowing it.

When it was clear that the students in Mrs W's class understood the concept, I showed a video without the sound. This technique was borrowed from Michelle Garcia Winner, also a Speech and Language Pathologist. She was known for developing a perspective sharing concept *Thinking About You, Thinking About Me*, a teaching tool for those with social cognitive deficits. The purpose of watching the video without words was to have the students rely on reading the body language of the characters in the video, using their own sixth sense. The exercise allowed them to realise for themselves how difficult it would be if a person had trouble identifying subtle non-verbal social cues. This was a fun technique that Thomas and I had practiced often. According to Mrs W, the presentation appeared to have a positive affect on her students. She said her class had been more compassionate toward Thomas after that presentation.

Second grade was a challenging year for Thomas as the academics were more difficult and the social expectations were higher. He demonstrated his frustration by melting down in response to the confusion. Mrs Trent discovered that she could engage Thomas in the lessons by becoming more creative and animated in her approach. She'd automatically use Thomas' special interest topics as a strategy to covey information for subjects that were difficult or particularly complex for him. She also became incredibly skilled at using redirection as a method for getting Thomas back on task.

Mrs W often called on Thomas to answer problems displayed by the overhead projector. Thomas loved the overhead projector. If a specific problem was difficult for him, Mrs W would talk him through it so that the class could see how smart he was. She'd deliberately ask him questions when she knew he'd know the answer. Because he was knowledgeable in science, she often called on him for help, noting it required a scientific brain. This served to build his self-esteem and to create an environment where his peers would acknowledge him for his strengths.

Despite all this bolstering, Thomas had numerous meltdowns that year. In response, the break card program was implemented. Five break-cards worth five minutes each were created especially for Thomas by a behaviorist on Thomas' IEP team, and were placed in his desk for easy access. It was a positive coping mechanism as well as a useful tool in addressing his anxiety. The program allowed Thomas to self-monitor and take a break when necessary without disrupting the class. In spite of all of this, Thomas made a great deal of academic progress in second grade. As so much attention was directed towards his expertise in science and art, Thomas also gained a lot of respect from his fellow classmates that year.

Near the end of that school year, I remember Thomas asking Mrs W if he could teach her class about the history of prehistoric dinosaurs. She generously agreed to a short presentation sometime before the end of the year. An hour before dismissal time on the last day of school, Thomas abruptly announced to Mrs W,

'Oh, I totally forgot about my presentation. Can I do it now?'

Keeping true to her word, she quickly collected her students and asked for their complete attention. As she introduced Thomas as a guest speaker, he proceeded with a factual presentation about the Triassic, Jurassic and Cretaceous periods. His classmates were interested, attentive and asked a number of questions at the end of his talk.

Summer after Second Grade

At the end of second grade, the long standing principal retired and a new principal arrived. Mrs Garton was young, full of energy and enjoyed young children. She was a breath of fresh air. She'd had a number of years experience in special education prior to taking her new role as principal. Thankfully, she stepped right in and worked well in collaboration with what the IEP team already had in place for Thomas.

In effect, due to her extensive knowledge about Special Education regulations and programs, Mrs Garton helped monitor an appropriate inclusion program for Thomas and other students requiring similar services. I realised right away that she was a skillful communicator who wasn't afraid to utilise resources that would improve the development and growth for Thomas and other students with similar issues. Her positive leadership and infectious optimism set her apart from others. She was extraordinary.

Third Grade

In third grade, the standard class size jumped from twenty children to thirty-four children. And even though Mrs Trent would continue as Thomas' aide, I was curious to know how the larger population and increased noise level would affect him. Mrs H had been teaching third grade for over twenty years and although she'd never before taught a child with Asperger's syndrome, she was open minded and interested in Thomas. She'd known him through previous teachers, and was prepared to learn the necessary skills to teach him in her classroom. Mrs H was a kind and compassionate person who taught her students the importance of caring for each other and to appreciate the differences in everyone. As a result, Thomas' classmates learned to recognise his triumphs and understand his challenges. Mrs Trent was especially helpful and remained the constant in his life at school. She continued using tactics that proved effective to keep Thomas engaged in a lesson. Many had grown to respect her knowledge, strategies and instructional techniques. In fact, as other children appeared with similar diagnoses, Mrs Trent was often asked for her insight.

Teaching the class about science

One of the third grade science units included learning about the Solar System. During a particular lesson, Mrs H was describing the planets while illustrating her points on the blackboard. In doing so, she inadvertently made an astronomy error and Thomas was quick to see it. From his chair he said, 'Excuse me Mrs H but I believe you've made an error regarding the Asteroid Belt.'

'Oh, you're absolutely correct, Thomas,' she said acknowledging her mistake and quickly correcting it. Thomas got up and stood beside her to co-teach the rest of the lesson. Again, Mrs H used that opportunity to show the class Thomas' understanding of the Solar System and they responded by applauding with great enthusiasm at the end. Later, Mrs H told me that not only was she impressed with his understanding of the planets, but also how comfortable he was at teaching his peers.

Fourth Grade

Academically and socially, the leap from third to fourth grade was immense; in addition, it was Ms E's first year as a teacher. Although Mrs Trent would continue as his aide, I was still a bit concerned about how Ms E would relate to Thomas. Just as I'd met with all of Thomas' previous teachers, I also met with Ms E prior to the start of school. As in earlier years, it was an opportunity for me to share information about AS, Thomas and the way he processed information. I felt that the curriculum shifted significantly in fourth grade and while Thomas was at grade level academically, with the exception of math, I knew it might be a hard year for both of them. As Thomas adjusted to Ms E and realised what was expected of him, Ms E challenged Thomas to rise up and achieve more. She encouraged Thomas to take-risks (her mantra). And he did!

Once he told her, 'I think math might be against my family's religion,' attempting to get out of a math quiz.

Ms E (same religion) replied, 'How weird, I've never heard that before. Did you know that you and I have the same religious background?'

Smiling, but quiet, Thomas quickly took his math quiz.

Thomas worked hard to become independent that year, while also expanding socially. Once, we were driving down the street and Thomas noticed a license plate that read, RISK TAKER.

'Mom, that car must belong to Ms E!' he said. Ms E had definitely made an impression on Thomas that year. He loved her!

Fifth Grade

By the time Thomas entered fifth grade, many teachers in the school knew who he was. Since second grade, I'd given several in-services to the entire school staff about Asperger's syndrome. The in-service request had been incorporated into his IEP, reflecting the need for AS education.

Thomas' fifth grade teacher was Mrs D. She loved teaching and had experience working as a resource teacher in prior years. Mrs D was patient, kind and a very structured teacher. Structure was great for Thomas and predictability was necessary for him to be successful in the classroom. As in previous years, Mrs D also recognised Thomas for his efforts in front of his peers. She understood that by emphasising his strengths and abilities, less attention was focused on the odd social behaviors that were demonstrated throughout his elementary school years. Modeling acceptance had been critically important in how he had been received by his peers over the years.

One of the highlights for Thomas in fifth grade was experiencing outdoor education. For three full days, three fifth grade classes met in the Santa Cruz Mountains to learn more about nature and the environment. When Thomas and I were considering if he'd go or not, Mrs D convinced us that Thomas should definitely have the experience. She was a devoted teacher and shared his love for science. That was the hook word – science. As a result, Thomas, his teacher, his aide, his principal and seventy other fifth graders from his school all had that wonderful memory to share. Autonomy was gained in fifth grade. Mrs D worked very hard to establish a safe environment where Thomas could learn to be responsible for himself and achieve independence. He grew tremendously in her class.

* * *

One winter day, as I picked up Thomas from school, we noticed a group of teachers, including Mrs D, huddled together in front of the school all dressed in black raincoats. I knew it was a deliberate and organised demonstration illustrating their disappointment regarding a no-increase in pay clause in their new teacher's agreement.

Curious about their attire, Thomas walked directly over to where they were. I followed but stood behind him. He asked the group why they were dressed in black. His fourth grade teacher, Ms E, immediately spoke up and told him it was because they were trying to make a point.

'What point?' Thomas questioned. She told him that all of the teachers wanted more money in their paycheck for being a teacher.

Thomas replied, 'You mean you get paid for this?' They all laughed, and then Mrs D explained that they needed to pay their bills too.

Thomas quickly offered, 'Well then, why don't you write a letter to your boss and ask for $100 more?' Again they laughed, but agreed it was a good idea.

With that, Thomas said goodbye and we walked away. Half way across campus, he abruptly turned around and yelled out to the group of teachers, 'You know what they say don't you?'

'What?' a few of them yelled back.

'Well, the ends justify the means!' They roared with laughter, and his fourth grade teacher declared, 'That's my student!' to which his fifth grade teacher replied, 'Actually, he's my student!'

If I were President

On Election Day, Thomas, along with all the other fifth grade students, was asked what he would do if he were the new President of the United States. He told his teacher, 'I would get rid of math for all the math haters.' Hearing this, I asked him why he wouldn't just 'get rid of math' for everyone.

His response? 'People should have a choice, Mom.'

He is his mother's child!

Thomas declares independence…

Declare Independence Essay

In the course of now, I, Mr. Thomas, declare independence from math. Most people think math and science are the same thing, when in real life, math and science are like oil and water. Math torments me. I know that science is 100% better than math.

I have this particular opinion about math because it's difficult for me, it confuses me and I just don't like it. Sometimes it even makes me turn into an out of control nut.

I think math stinks. I think that I can become a great scientist without math. If math was a guy, I think it would look like someone who has his mouth on a stalk and his eye balls pulled out of its sockets.

I officially declare independence from math!

'So long math,' Thomas bellows, laughing hysterically.

The night before the United States presidential election Thomas had been interested in certain aspects of the presidential election. He was curious about the candidates, their different viewpoints and their political positions. Specifically, he wanted to know who had the decision making powers and why. He'd watched some of the presidential debates with me on television, but said most of it was 'boring'. He was, however, anxious to know who would be the next President of the United States. The night before the election, Thomas asked me how many miles there were between California and Washington DC. When I asked him why, he said, 'I was hoping to tell the winner of the election something.'

'What would you tell him?'

'Well, if President Bush won, I would ask him to spend more money on educating children,' Thomas told me.

'What would you ask Senator Kerry if he were to win the election?' I asked.

'I wouldn't ask him anything,' Thomas said matter of factly. 'I would just say congratulations!' In the morning following the election, Thomas watched the morning news with me. It was reported that President Bush had won and would be assuming his role of President for a second term. Thomas started to cry. He said he was sad that George W. Bush would be ruling the U.S. again. When I asked why, he said, 'Mr. Kerry was the one who said he would give money to the schools for education.' I assured him that Mr. Bush would too, most likely.

Fifth Grade assignment

Thomas' teacher incorporated public speaking and book reviews as part of the language arts curriculum in her fifth grade class. To practice organisation of thought, she required her students to write letters to her each month. As a guide, at the beginning of each month she wrote a letter to all of her students. In return, she requested that they each write a letter back to her on the assigned topic and in similar format. Thomas was able to parlay his 'restricted interests' into productive assignments. The following are examples of those assignments.

January 4, 2005

Dear Mrs D,

I enjoyed reading your letter this month. I think I am a smart student. Because of this, I find that most things are easy for me. However, there are two things about me that you should know. I think math and homework 'are the crab grass of life'. That means, 'It's ugly and it can pop up anywhere'. I try to study a lot before a test. I usually try and memorise facts, but sometimes I forget them. I think my strength is memorisation, usually.

I am excited about becoming a future film maker. I enjoy the fact that you can make movies that are exciting for people to watch. Did you know that you can become famous by making films that people think are very intriguing? I intend to continue school (middle school through college), so that I can become a famous film maker. If I do become a famous film maker one day, I will always remember you (Mrs D) as the 5th grade teacher that taught me everything.

Sincerely,

TJB

February 6, 2005

Dear Mrs D,

I am a very good scriptwriter. For my daily typing project, I am writing a script. I'm currently writing a sequel on the Yu-Gi-Oh movie. It's not an original idea. Usually, I enjoy script writing because I can create the characters and new ideas that fit into my story. Script writing can sometimes lead to a hit movie. I think that's exciting.

Writing is important in life because it's a way to express new ideas. It's actually a way of communicating without talking. Of course, there is always sign language as an alternative.

Sincerely,

TJB

March 10, 2005

Dear Mrs D,

My favorite sport is where you kick your legs and paddle your arms at the same time, otherwise known as swimming. I was on a swim team called the Barracudas for two years in a row. Swimming allowed me to explore close spaces in water. However, I could only swim in swimming pools because I couldn't seem to fit into a sink or glass of water. I am just kidding! Gotcha!

I learned that kicking your feet while swimming propels you through the water. I also think swimming is very fun. In the future, I plan to coach a swimming team and swim into even deeper water myself. I received several blue ribbons for completing my Barracuda swim team. I like swimming in the summer.

Sincerely,

TJB

April 9, 2005

Dear Mrs D,

First, I am going to tell you what I did this year for spring break. My Mom and I went to the beach. We stayed in a room at a house, known as a 'bed and breakfast'. In the living room, they had a library of videos. I borrowed the movie Jurassic Park.

We also went to the Monterey Bay Aquarium and saw a great white shark. It's the only one in captivity. I also went to a store near the beach and bought a quarter that's never been circulated. That means it's never been used by anyone. I had fun!

My ideal spring break would be spending a week inside of a zoo with genetically engineered dinosaurs, called Cretaceous Park. All the dinosaurs would be made from bird and lizard DNA. (Doesn't that sound familiar?) I would be the zoo operator and my Mom would be the zookeeper. All the kid visitors would be able to have a pet dinosaur, a little version of their own favorite dinosaur. Wouldn't this be a great idea for a movie?

Sincerely,

TJB

May 6, 2005

Dear Mrs D,

I'm kind of anxious about going to middle school because it will be a new school with new people. I'm also excited about it because I'll be a cool sixth grader. My goal in the future is simply to learn. I hope I can eventually learn to movie-make and become the coolest and most creative movie director the world has ever known.

I hope I can go to ID Tech camp again this summer or next summer. That's where they teach kids how to make movies. Last summer I made a movie called Family Blackout. A group of us put our ideas together with music and made a DVD movie.

I think that when I'm 13 years old I will go to a summer camp at Stanford University to learn how to make digital effects for my movies. You have to be 13 years old to attend.

Sincerely,

TJB

Saturday, March 12, 2005

Dearest Thomas,

This is so exciting to be able to write you a letter! It is exciting for many reasons; first, you're usually the one writing letters to me and now I have the opportunity to write to you. Second, this letter comes to you at a really exciting time in your life. You're moving on as they would say, you're growing up, you're off to great places, and you're off and away (I'm going to steal some words from Dr. Seuss if you don't mind).

The move from elementary school to middle school is a ginormous step in your life. (I don't want to use the word big!) You're going to be switching classes, having a lot of teachers, having lots of homework (sorry), making new friends and keeping your old ones! You're going to experience a lot of new and exciting things. The world is going to open up more for you. This means that all your knowledge is going grow even huge-er!

Thomas, it has been such a joy to have you in my D-4 5th grade class. You have brought many insightful pieces of knowledge to my life and you have made me chuckle along the way. You are a strong reader, an amazing writer with incredible voice, a super scientist, an influential public speaker, a superior speller, an astounding artist, and… well I won't mention anything about math in this letter].

I remember this one time you were trying to come into the classroom in the morning with your backpack. I said to you, 'Thomas, you need to take your things out of your backpack, leave your backpack against the wall, and then come into the classroom.' You then replied (hand to forehead with a grunt noise) 'Drat, I'm a slave to routine.' I thought this was a funny way to start my day, and it made me realise, hey, I too am a slave to routine and wouldn't it be wonderful to take a break from that routine every now and then? Well, what a great thing it is going to be summer time before we know it.

As I write this letter, I'm also remembering the time we went to Outdoor School. It was probably scary for you to make that decision, but you did and I know you were so thankful! I was able to watch you become more independent and soak up all the nature around you. Whenever I saw you hiking or tide pooling you had a look on your face that said to me, 'I never want this to end'. As a teacher that is a look you want to see from your students. I was so proud of you during that entire week. You took many courageous steps and that confirmed in my mind how brave you are!

Speaking of proud… I could never tell you enough how proud of you I am! You have worked so hard in 5th grade, you have never given up and you have persevered through some hard times. I hope you will be able to look back to 5th grade and think to yourself, 'Wow, I learned a lot; it definitely prepared me for middle school, and I had so much fun along the way!'

Thomas, always remember that I'm close by if you ever need to talk or vent or ask for advice. You have to promise you won't forget me and that you'll visit and tell me of all your adventures.

I will miss you… Your 5th grade teacher, Mrs D

Misunderstanding

When Thomas was in fifth grade, I received a note from Thomas' Resource Teacher (RS). It explained how Thomas was part of a math group that met twice a week. Thomas struggled in math and I expected this would be an opportunity for him to improve his math skills in a social setting. As I read further, the resource teacher wrote how well Thomas worked independently and how he interacted with his peers appropriately.

The very end of the note concluded with how an incident had occurred involving Thomas. The note described Thomas as becoming angry at one point in the session, stating to the entire group, 'I wish I could slap you like dorks.' The note to me ended with, 'Just thought you should know...'

Thomas had been working with that particular RS for two years. I was curious to know what Thomas thought of that very same incident. I asked Thomas if he had commented to his math group, 'I wish I could slap you like dorks'? He said, 'No. I said, I wish I could slam you like doors. I was very angry because they were all talking at once. I just wanted to shut them out.'

In addition, the RS indicated that Thomas had written something negative about another student on a note. When I asked him if this were true, he started to cry. He said that another student had written that negative comment about the other student. He said, 'I told Miss F the truth but she didn't believe me. I was so offended!'

With that, I quickly called the RS. I spoke to her about her note and what Thomas had told me. I asked her if she had actually heard Thomas say, 'I wish I could slap you like dorks.' To my surprise she said she had. I asked her if she could have heard him say, 'I want to slam you like doors'? She told me it was possible. In fact, she agreed that actually that sentence made more sense in the context of what had occurred.

I asked her if she had examined the 'hand writing' on the negative comment written on a note. She said she thought she had. I told her that Thomas told me that he did not write the note, and that he'd explained to her who had. After carefully examining the note, I told her that I was impressed with the handwriting. I quickly reminded her that Thomas had terrible motor control and couldn't write evenly. In fact, it was one of the reasons he worked with her in Resource. I told her I would send back the note for her to review it again. Then she told me that she didn't really think Thomas had written the note and that she would talk to him the next day. I asked Thomas if he wanted to speak to her on the telephone to discuss this matter further. He loudly replied, 'No! She offended me!' She hung up after again apologising to me for the misunderstanding, and agreed to pursue the matter further with the other student and his parents.

Note: The following day, Thomas' aide confirmed that the words written on the note were not written in Thomas' handwriting. When the RS called together the same group of students, finally one confessed to writing the negative note and Thomas demanded an apology.

The point of this story is to illustrate that in spite of the background of the RS and her familiarity with Thomas, she reacted before carefully considering the facts in the situation, as many of us do. This, of course, is not to say that Thomas can't be wrong, inappropriate or overreact sometimes. In fact, quite often he misunderstands or assumes a false perception of a situation (like in the next story). He does however, have a strong sense of right and wrong and will defend himself when necessary.

Noticing the difference

One day I received a phone call from my son's principal saying, 'It's not a huge deal, but I thought you should know that there was an incident involving Thomas at recess today.' Then she went on to explain how a little boy had been grabbed around his neck by Thomas during the morning recess. Evidently, a fourth grade little boy somehow accidentally stepped on Thomas' hand while playing at recess and in response Thomas grabbed him around his throat. The little boy was frightened and Thomas was very upset.

Apparently, when the incident occurred, Thomas immediately mentioned it to his aide saying that, 'A boy stepped on my hand and it hurt'. He was visibly upset and his aide tried to comfort him, not aware that Thomas had in turn reacted to the other child.

That evening, I spoke to Thomas about the incident and his reaction to it. He was still troubled by the episode, which led us into a discussion about appropriate actions and alternative behaviors. He told me that he'd sometimes felt like he was out of control. He said that he'd wished he had a normal brain so that he wouldn't feel so impulsive at times. When I asked him what he meant, he said he had an Asperger's brain and it was different. He was crying and told me that he wanted to be like everyone else. He didn't like feeling different, 'Even if it means that I won't be a famous or legendary film maker [his dream], I'd rather just be normal sometimes,' he told me.

We hadn't before discussed how it felt to him to have Asperger's syndrome. We'd only talked about what it was and that he had it. I sympathised with how it must be difficult to feel out of control sometimes, 'I feel like that too at times,' I shared. Silently, I considered how hard it must be to feel so frustrated and isolated and to be aware of the reason, yet not completely understand it.

We fell into a conversation about how the brain typically developed and how genetically everyone was different. I rattled off a list of his incredible gifts and talents and told him how special I thought he was. I tried to cheer him up but truthfully it stung to know he felt so bad. By the end of our conversation he seemed better, but it was very hard for me to witness his realisation. I saw him as a brilliant, incredibly kind and caring young person. It seemed unfair that he should suffer from a neurobiological difference affecting many aspects of his life, and at times take a negative perspective of himself.

Letters to Thomas from his teachers and other adults helped to give him some positive messages about himself. They are included on the following pages.

March 20, 2005

Dear Thomas,

Wow! I can't believe that you are in fifth grade now. I've been your helper since you were in kindergarten; that's five years, almost half your life! And soon you'll be going to middle school…you are so grown up.

I remember when you were in kindergarten. I was so amazed at what a talented artist you were. You would draw these fabulous trains with faces on them. In first grade, you were one of the top readers in the class. I thought, 'he is so smart!' When you were in second grade, you used to love to sit next to Mrs W when she read stories to the class. And I remember when she called you up to the overhead projector to do a math problem with tens blocks. And in front of the whole class you did a division problem, explaining each step like you were some kind of a math genius!!

Third grade was the year that you started on the road to independence. You started typing your work on the computer. You would dictate wonderful stories to me and I just loved listening to them. I remember when Mrs H was teaching the lesson on the solar system and you helped teach the class about the asteroid belt. I thought, 'he is brilliant!'

You became even more independent in forth grade. You did more of your own writing and typing. Whenever Miss E would call on you to answer a question, you were always correct. And I thought, 'Can he get any smarter?'

Well, I guess so, because here we are in fifth grade and you are Mr. Independent. You go through each day needing little help from me or Mrs D. You are a whiz at Language Arts and Social Studies and try harder than any kid I know at math. And science, well, the only word that comes to mind is genius!

Definitely a highlight for me this year was going to camp with you. You are a great cabin buddy. My favorite part was going on the forest hike with you. I remember when we went on the card hike and one of the cards said to make a wish for the earth. And you said, 'My wish for the earth is that it can defend itself against the growing population.' Wow! I was so amazed that you said that because there wasn't anything more perfect to say. I will never forget the experience of going to camp with you, Thomas. It was one of the highlights of my entire life. Thinking back over the past five years, there are so many great memories of you. The great stories that you wrote, the incredible drawings, and of course hanging out with you on field trips. But mostly I think of the kind of person you are; kind and thoughtful, smart and funny, artistic and talented and… brilliant! I know that whatever you choose to do when you grow up, a paleontologist or a movie director (or both) you will be successful. You've accomplished so much in the past five years. I can't wait to find out what you'll accomplish when you get to middle school. You'll do great!

Fondly,

Mrs Trent

April 3, 2005

Dear Thomas,

Can you find how many idioms there are in this letter?

As I write this letter to you, I have a smile on my face. Do you know why? Because I'm thinking about you, and when I'm thinking about you, it makes me happy.

It all began August 28th 2003. I was at school for my first official day of work. There weren't any students around because school hadn't started. I was working in my room when over the loud speaker I heard Mrs Garton say she needed the speech and resource teachers in the office. My first thoughts were, 'Why am I being sent to the principal's office? What could I possibly have done wrong when I hadn't even worked an entire school day?' My heart started pounding and I had butterflies in my stomach as I neared the office. Then Mrs Garton introduced me to the Resource Teacher. She had a smile on her face so she seemed nice and friendly. There was another woman there who had a cup of joe in her hand (It was your Mom. I immediately thought I would like her because I like coffee too, especially Starbucks.) Also, there was a boy as cute as a button named Thomas. I remembered hearing that name before. The previous speech teacher told me of this very special boy that I would get to work with. She said she enjoyed working with him and that he was the cat's meow.

When we met, I knew we were going to hit it off immediately. I love to be around people who have a sense of humor and I can't remember what you said to me, but you cracked me up and that made me feel good inside. Mrs Garton made me laugh also, so I figured that this school might just be a good place to work.

When school started, I was curious about starting to work with you. I had never worked with anyone who had Asperger's syndrome (not Asperger's Disorder, duh!). I had experience working with children with social thinking issues, but I knew I had a lot to learn about Asperger's. See, I know that I'm your Speech Therapist and my job is to teach you about thinking about others, but I have news for you. You have taught me so much about thinking about others. Now you may be thinking to yourself, 'Hold your horses lady, you're supposed to be the teacher.' But honestly, you have been the teacher in many cases. You taught me to think outside the box in how I socialise with people and how I need to think about how others are thinking. I never realised until I met you that some people just have a different way about thinking about others (or not thinking about others – whichever the case may be!) I recall a conversation I had with you while you were teasing one of your speech partners, in a friendly teasing sort of way – not mean spirited teasing. This is how the conversation went:

Thomas: 'I get 4 stickers and he only gets 3.'

Me: 'No way, Jose.'

Thomas: 'Yes I do!'

Me: 'In your dreams!'

Thomas: 'In my reality.'

I know you were just teasing when you said, 'In my reality', but it really made me think about how some people think of reality different than others.

I know sometimes I drive you up a wall while working on having conversations with people. Remember the time we were talking with Mrs Garton in my room and you just blurted out, 'I'm done with this conversation. I've had enough!'? Mrs Garton laughed so hard because we can all relate to conversations that we don't want to be in, but we don't say it! That might make the person feel bad! Houston, we have a problem, someone just made a social blunder, get out the rubber chicken and bonk him on the head!

One of my favorite quotes from you comes from when we were talking about what you were going to be for Halloween. You told me you were going to be the Grim Reaper and I said, 'You can't be the Grim Reaper you're too nice to be the Grim Reaper!' and you commented, 'Too nice looking, but looks can deceive.'

As I think of you going off to middle school I have a mix of emotions. I am excited for you that you are moving on and growing up. But on the other hand, I get so sad thinking about not being able to work with you next year. I don't know who will enjoy being bonked on the head with a rubber chicken as much as you have! Middle school is lucky to be getting such a smart, intelligent, nice guy like you. Now when you get there, don't bite off more than you can chew or get beside yourself. Just cool it.

When you're walking down the hallways of your new school, remember me and the main thing we worked on…thinking about others just like you know. I'll be thinking about you.

I'll really miss you and your sense of humor.

Blessings,

Ms R.

March 11, 2005

Dear Thomas,

Your mom has asked me to write you a letter, so that you can look back on your years in elementary school with fond memories. This is such a time of change for both you and me. I am moving to a new state with a new job, and you are rapidly growing and will move on to middle school. I have so many wonderful memories of you over the last three years that I have been principal here. I think it's sad, but some principals don't ever get to know their students like I know you.

When I first met you, you were in the third grade. I remember several instances when you became frustrated. I was always able to reason with you, and I loved your sense of fairness. Remember when you modeled the correct way to make brownies for your class? We videotaped it so that your Uncle Marc could see you in school. You spoke loudly so that everyone could hear you, and you worked hard to make eye contact with your audience. It was a great moment to see. Third grade was the year I showed you that I had gel pens in my office, and that they were available for your use whenever you wanted them. You loved all the beautiful colors, and drew me many of your incredibly detailed drawings of everything from dinosaurs to Bionicle characters. You are so artistically talented. This was what created the safe and comfortable space that you enjoyed in my office. Oh, how many times you stealthily moved past the office staff to sit in the same chair you loved each day. Of course, they always saw you, but knew that you and I had a silent agreement. Truth be told, they loved you too.

Fourth grade proved to be a year of change. So many more kids in your class, and more difficult work was added. Stability continued to be provided in the office, and you continued to visit at lunch. What most stands out for me that year was when you told me that you were going to be writing and producing a new movie. You asked me if you could use the multi use room for auditions and the performance. I said, 'Perhaps.' You sat in my office and created posters to announce the auditions. For days following I kept finding your audition posters all over the school walls. This event still makes me chuckle. Probably the most profound visit from you came when I was hospitalised. You entered my room with a, 'Hi!' I'm not sure if the IV's scared you or not, but you appeared to keep your distance. The visit was touching and quite reassuring for me.

Now here you are in the last stretch of fifth grade. Still you continue to make me think, and laugh often. Just after giving my resignation and notification to the students, you were sitting in my office during your usual time. You were sitting in my chair; this was very unusual, as you had a self-designated assigned seat. On this occasion, in my chair, someone asked you what you were doing. You responded quite confidently,

'I am the principal.' The teacher pointed out that I was still the principal, and you reminded her, 'Then I will be the principal at the end of the month when Mrs Garton leaves.'

I once told your mother that I believed that you always felt safe in my office. This safety allowed you to say and feel whatever. Recently, I came into my office while you were eating your lunch. I had been held up in a very long meeting that ran into the lunch hour. I told you that I was so hungry that my tummy was growling. You replied full of disgust, 'Your stomach?' I asked why you corrected me and you clarified, 'If you were brilliant like me, you would use scientific vocabulary.' What a great laugh for me. Perhaps you were correct.

I will always think about your time at outdoor school. You had such a great time, and you learned a lot. I remember how emotional you got at fireside time. 'I have become so attached to this outdoor school,' you whined through tears. I will miss your visits. I did not always get to see you when you came to my office. I did, however, know that you had been there. A little food wrapper or juice box straw wrapper would be the only remnants of your visit. You are an intelligent, funny, beautiful child. I will always remember you.

Fondly,

Mrs Garton

Principal

Chapter Three

Resources

Insurance eligibility

Disillusioned is the word I would use to describe the initial feeling I had as a parent following Thomas' diagnosis of an Autistic Spectrum Disorder. The news was life changing. Suddenly, like many parents in that situation, I was forced to think about the prognosis and immediately projected my son's future. When the diagnosis finally sank in, I realised that I needed to get moving and make things happen.

There were no road maps to follow about who, what, where, when or how to choose which services and why. Therefore, I initially found those decisions extremely difficult to make and prioritise. Although I was referred to several agencies, what I quickly learned was that many of the services that were said to be useful and necessary for a child on the spectrum were often not immediately available for various reasons.

An example: when Thomas was six and a half, I searched for a psychologist who had experience working with children on the autistic spectrum. I contacted twenty-seven different professionals in my HMO plan and not one of them had an opening. Then I found Clare who agreed to meet with Thomas weekly. This was important because it provided a structured setting where Thomas could express himself naturally, and where she could effectively address his specific issues. Dr. Clare worked with Thomas through play therapy, focusing on key aspects of his emotional and social development and how it related to his diagnosis. After six months, I began to see Thomas progress in areas of self-awareness and in his self-monitoring capabilities. This was encouraging.

At that point in time, though I had been submitting Dr. Clare's weekly doctor's visits to his health insurance company, I'd routinely receive explanations of benefits from the insurance company denying reimbursement. I was told that his insurance company didn't cover psychotherapy for autism under his current policy.

This was difficult for me to understand as I knew autism was considered to be a neurobiological disorder, that is, a medical condition. I requested the actual policy, which they promptly provided, and I reviewed thoroughly. It was correct. According to his insurance policy, psychotherapy was not listed as one of the health benefits for the diagnosis of autism.

However, through research, I discovered that a new Assembly Bill (AB 88) had been recently passed in the state of California. It directly applied to 'mental health coverage' including autism and had been effective as of July 1, 2000. I quickly informed my son's insurance company about AB 88, while attaching a detailed copy of his medical diagnosis. The summary of this Bill:

Requires the coverage for the diagnosis and treatment of severe mental illness in people of all ages and serious emotional disturbances of children, as defined under the same terms and conditions applicable to medical conditions.

This included Pervasive Developmental Disorder or Autism.

Note: Shortly thereafter, Thomas' health insurance company began reimbursement for his weekly visits with Dr. Clare.

RCEB story

At the age of three, Thomas was given the diagnosis of Pervasive Developmental Disorder (PDD), an Autistic Spectrum Disorder. Then at age six, he was assessed again and I was told by his doctor that Thomas' characteristics, development and behaviors were more consistent with a diagnosis of Asperger's syndrome, also an Autistic Spectrum Disorder. After extensively researching the new AS diagnosis, I was referred to the Regional Center of the East Bay (RCEB). I was told that Thomas may be eligible for certain services.

It emerged that respite was available for parents who have children with autism. When Thomas was about six and a half, I sought services for respite care through the RCEB. I quickly learned that certain protocol and criteria needed to be followed before he could actually qualify for services through the RCEB.

At the time, the RCEB contracted with Children's Hospital to verify and or diagnose autism. Consequently, the RCEB would then approve or deny services based on the recommendations made by the clinicians from Children's Hospital. I was told that for me to qualify for respite based on Thomas' autism diagnosis, another assessment would be required. I later learned that part of the assessment was subjective, making the decision for services individually based.

It was around three o'clock in the afternoon when Thomas and I arrived at Children's Hospital for his assessment appointment. I was immediately introduced to the psychologist who promptly explained to me that the assessment would have two parts. She informed me that part one would take about three hours. Part two was scheduled for the following day and took about the same length of time. I was then introduced to a medical doctor, who was apparently the director of the assessment program. The three of us sat in a room, while I was asked to give chronological facts about Thomas' developmental history. Both doctors enquired a lot about his current abilities and deficits. I supplied an enormous amount of information, in addition to explaining which services he had received. I explained to them that I attributed much of his progress directly to the Speech and Language therapy, occupational therapy, physical therapy, adapted P.E., social skills programs and psychotherapy that he had received, and continued to receive. The psychologist nodded and appeared to record it in her notes.

The MD shook my hand and walked away, stating she had another patient to see. Shortly there after, the psychologist told Thomas it was his turn. He had been stacking cups on the floor and rummaging through the toy chest during our discussion.

'I don't think Thomas will be able to test for three hours without frequent breaks,' I told the psychologist. She smiled at me, but didn't respond.

Again, I politely noted that in an effort to obtain accurate results (since services were at stake), I suggested breaks might be necessary for Thomas. I knew there would be no way she would be able to get him to answer questions, verbally or otherwise, for an extended length of time without a break. Again, the psychologist smiled at me, but said nothing. I wondered if she heard me.

She probably heard that sentiment all the time from parents, but because she didn't seem to acknowledge my concern, I stooped down to Thomas and looked him right in the face. 'Here are some snacks for you in case you get hungry. If you need a break, just tell the lady that. I will be right outside,' I told him.

Then, I turned to the psychologist and said, 'He didn't eat much because we had to rush right over here from school.' She nodded her head (this seemed to register), and then she asked Thomas to stay with her so she could talk to him.

I had been telling Thomas about this appointment for several days. I had explained to him that a person would be asking him questions, describing situations and telling him stories. I also explained that the person would then ask him questions about what they talked about.

To confirm his diagnosis of Asperger's syndrome, I knew that the information they obtained from him needed to be accurate, and I hoped it would be.

About 40 minutes later, Thomas came running out of the room. He said his brain was tired. I told him he could have a snack and take a break. Ten minutes later, the psychologist whisked him back into the room to continue the assessment. Twenty minutes after that, he again came running out of the room and sat next to me. I told him he could rest for a while. The psychologist asked him to return. He ignored her and held my hand. I told him he could take a break and then he needed to finish up with the lady.

Ten minutes later, he went with her to finish up. He held himself together for about another twenty minutes before he ran out of the room again. I told the psychologist that we were done for the day. Clearly, he was done! We returned the following day for much of the same type of testing. Tests and breaks for him, while I sat outside of the room and waited curiously.

Finally after about three hours of that, the psychologist walked out and said she was done. Although she said she would send me the written assessment when it was ready, she did offer me some information.

She said, 'Ms Barber, I don't think Thomas has Asperger's syndrome.'

'Really!' What do you think he has?' I was flabbergasted.

'I think he has a number of different issues going on. I think perhaps he has an anxiety disorder, maybe a compulsive disorder, and definitely some sort of language impairment,' she explained.

I was at a lost for words. Not because I agreed with her, but because I didn't.

'Trust me,' I told her. 'There's no one who wants to agree with you more than me right now, but I don't believe you're accurate. Based on my experiences with him, his developmental history, his autistic like characteristics and a previous AS diagnosis, in addition to my own extensive knowledge in this field, I believe my son to have Asperger's.'

I couldn't believe it. It made me question her experience and familiarity with diagnosing children with Asperger's syndrome. I was curious to know exactly how many children she had diagnosed appropriately with having Asperger's? She didn't respond to my obvious difference of opinion. In fact, I believe she was offended that I challenged her final impression of my son.

She stared at me and slowly shook her head back and forth finally stating, 'I'm sorry, but because he doesn't meet the criteria (autistic criteria), he automatically does not qualify for any service with RCEB.'

Oh, then it became clear. Whew! For a minute, I thought I was losing my mind.

'That's interesting!' I told her. I quickly asked, 'If you had found him to have Asperger's (as previously diagnosed by a Neurodevelopmental Pediatrician), would he then qualify for respite services under their current criteria?'

'Of course!' the psychologist replied.

'I see! Thank you for your time,' I said. And with that, Thomas and I turned and walked out of the building together without saying another word.

The next morning, I contacted the intake coordinator from the Regional Center. I had been communicating with him by telephone for a number of months prior to scheduling the assessment date. He had been helpful, but this time he referred me to his supervisor. I spoke to the supervisor at length. I told her that I had strongly disagreed with the psychologist's assessment of Thomas. I also told her that I understood that based on the psychologist's latest diagnosis of him that he would be denied respite services through the RCEB. The supervisor confirmed the information. I told her that I intended to appeal that decision, even though the results were verbal and had not yet been recorded.

After some discussion, the supervisor asked if I would agree to yet another assessment to determine eligibility. This time, she offered an independent psychologist in private practice. It was a psychologist who was well respected and whose reputation I was very familiar with. I thanked her and told her that I would consider the offer.

In the meantime, I researched Developmental Disabilities Services on the internet. I quickly found information about the Lanterman Developmental Disabilities Service Act. This was a California Law that was passed in 1969, and was associated with the RCEB. I contacted my Congressperson and requested a copy of that Act. I discovered that that law specifically promised services and support for those who were developmentally disabled. But most importantly, I learned that all Regional Centers received State Funding to provide those specific services under the Lanterman Act. Autism was considered to be one of those developmental disabilities. I also discovered that the RCEB used the Diagnostic Statistical Manuel (DSM IV) criteria to determine eligibility for services based on a diagnosis of autism. I later learned that a revised DSM IV version, more loosely written, was referenced.

I eventually contacted the supervisor at the RCEB. I mentioned to her that I had researched quite extensively the particulars of the Lanterman Act. I also pointed out that the criteria the RCEB used to determine eligibility for services (DSM IV), had a new and revised version. Then, I agreed to another assessment of Thomas with a new psychologist. (Note: Thomas' individual psychotherapist strongly felt Thomas indeed had AS, and encouraged me to have him re-tested.)

This time, I sat in the room with Thomas and the psychologist the entire time. Again, I gave his complete developmental history and a list of the services that have helped him progress. We spoke at length about Thomas' social deficit and how diligently he had worked to enhance that ability. I shared with her various strategies that were, and still are, useful in broadening his list of special interests. Although predictability was extremely important to Thomas, I shared with her that becoming less rigid and more 'flexible' in his everyday life was something we continued to work on. I explained that although he had made tremendous progress since his initial autism diagnosis at the age of three, his areas of need were still quite apparent.

She observed him carefully, while he responded to a series of questions. Part of the testing included the ADOS test, which I later learned was particularly useful in diagnosing autism. Following several hours and many breaks for Thomas, the psychologist completed the assessment of him. She told me I could expect the written results from her within two weeks. I stood staring at her. Then, she leaned toward me and softly said, 'There is no doubt in my mind that your son has Asperger's syndrome. I've been doing this a long time and although he has some extreme deficits, he has a lot of potential. You have done an amazing job with him and with continued services; I can't wait to see what he'll become.' I smiled and thanked her for her assessment.

Two weeks later I received her written report reflecting her comments. I started receiving respite services for Thomas through the RCEB immediately.

Note: Just as parents must rely heavily on professional input, it's equally important to rely on the information believed to be inherently correct.

Gluten free Casein free diet

When Thomas was about six, I noticed that he was easily distracted. He was 'spacey' and it became hard for him to stay on topic or maintain a connected conversation. About that time, I remembered reading an article from a parent's magazine about the gluten free and casein free (GFCF) diet, and how it had been used in children with autism. Gluten is an ingredient found in several grains while casein is the protein found in cow's milk. I was intrigued by the concept that a diet could actually 'lessen the fog' in terms of attention, which led me into researching the GFCF diet and the theory behind it. I discovered that some people were severely affected by the presence of gluten and or casein in their system. Many exhibited physical signs, including extreme gastrointestinal probleMs Although Thomas' pediatrician wasn't convinced that it would make a significant difference in his attention or behavior, I tried it anyway.

Though I was excited about the possibilities, I was still somewhat apprehensive. By altering Thomas' diet I was concerned that he wouldn't receive the nutrients that he needed. By essentially eliminating all casein, gluten, wheat, whey, barley, oats and rye, I worried about the reduced vitamins and minerals. I sought consultation with a nutritionist before proceeding with this new diet plan, who suggested simultaneously adding vitamins and other foods rich in the essential nutrients.

According to the literature I read, the recommendation was to eliminate one thing at a time. First I stopped all casein in Thomas' diet. This was done to determine which foods had an effect, if any, on his ability to focus. At that point, he'd been drinking more than half a gallon of milk every day since the age of three. I logged each meal in a food diary, documenting my observation of his moods, attention level, behaviors and his ability to concentrate.

Limited by textures, Thomas was resistant to the new foods and routine. He was tactilely defensive and was completely resistant to the food change. Prior to the GFCF diet, he'd relied on a mealtime routine with the consistency of familiar foods. This was a big deal. Although structure and predictability were necessary for Thomas, I knew he was a logical thinker. When I explained to him why this change might benefit him, he eventually agreed to label reading as a first step. As any good detective would, he checked every ingredient listed on foods he wanted, as well as the foods I wanted.

I introduced a new food each week. My only request was that he'd try two bites of each new food when offered. He didn't have to swallow it, just taste it. He agreed. Three months passed before I noticed that he seemed to focus better, and it wasn't long after that before his teachers remarked on his improved attentiveness in class. They also commented that he appeared more aware of himself. While there was some change after eliminating gluten, it was not as obvious as it was with casein.

Today, Thomas continues to be GFCF. He's attempted several times to include gluten and casein into his diet on separate occasions, but has said he feels better on the GFCF diet. Being a creature of habit, still today he checks food labels before trying anything new.

Making math real

Thomas has difficulty with symbol imagery. By that I mean he often doesn't see the relationship between numbers, which makes understanding math, even at its lowest level, extremely difficult for him.

By the beginning of fifth grade, double digit addition and subtraction, multiplication and division were expected to have been understood. Unfortunately for Thomas, he hadn't yet mastered that, nor had he completely memorised his multiplication facts. This was interesting to me, as I knew he'd learned his math facts through song, up to twelve, by the second grade. He would sing the entire song all the way through, over and over again, and I thought it was a great way to learn. What I didn't realise was that if he were asked a specific multiplication fact, other than the obvious zero, ones, fives and tens, he'd have to sing the entire song until he reached the fact that was asked about. By the fifth grade this was an obvious issue and it needed to be addressed.

The resource program offered by the school district had not been effective, so I took Thomas to a private educator who assessed his basic math skills. The results confirmed that Thomas had a symbol imagery problem and he was referred to a specific math programme called Making Math Real. The programme taught math using a multi-sensory approach. Their concept addressed the underlying developmental issues that supported the acquisition of basic math tools. He started this programme right away.

Following several one-on-one sessions using this new approach, Thomas began to understand and identify with the relationship between numbers. For the first time in his life he felt successful in learning math. The strategies used in this program focused on the teaching as well as the methodologies. Fabulous!

As part of this program and to encourage learning and participation, each student was offered to be part of a reward system. Thomas loved this idea! Once, following a particularly productive math session, Thomas was given a prize. While his tutor and I discussed his session, I felt him put his 'prize' in my coat pocket. Later, and as a special treat, Thomas and I went to the Lawrence Hall of Science. This was two blocks from his math tutor and one of his most favorite places to visit. They had many interactive science projects and interesting exhibits. As regular customers we often made it a point to visit the science store on the way out of the museum. On that day, I noticed an unusual looking die near the check out counter. It was clear with a tiny blue die inside of it. I thought it was interesting and showed it to Thomas. He liked it too. Later, when we'd arrived home I took off my coat and noticed something in my pocket. It was a clear die with a tiny blue die inside of it. Surprised, I held it in my hand and yelled out to Thomas. He immediately came over and looked at the die I was holding.

'It's not what you think, Mom!' He said firmly, staring straight into my eyes.

Wow, I'd never thought I would hear him say, 'I know what you're thinking.'

He struggled with perspective taking.

'What do I think?' I asked him.

'You think this is the same die you showed me from the science store. But, it isn't! Karen [his math tutor] gave me the die you're holding for my prize today,' he declared matter of factly.

Really?' I questioned, thinking it would be unlike him to take something without paying for it. Still, I thought it was quite a coincidence.

'If it bothers you, you can ask Karen about it,' he suggested, and walked out of the room.

A few weeks later, I retold the story to Karen, who was quick to verify Thomas' version as being nothing but absolutely accurate. Although I was happy to hear the truth confirmed, I was more thrilled to hear Thomas say he knew what I was thinking without me having to say a word.

Note: Between the ages of two and a half and eleven, Thomas has improved tremendously in a number of areas. Along with his determination and willingness to learn, I attribute much of his success to the ongoing private resources he'd received. They included: pragmatic speech therapy, occupational therapy, social skills classes, positive behavior therapy, tutoring in concept imagery and psychotherapy – not to mention school resources and the outside extra curricular activities he'd participated in.

Chapter Four

Borrowed Text

Sarcasm

It's often thought that children with AS are serious by nature and have no sense of humour. This may or may not be true; when describing anyone, general statements don't always apply. Although Thomas doesn't always get subtle jokes and some sarcasm, he does have the ability to be sarcastic himself. It's definitely learned sarcasm or what I call 'borrowed text'. Nevertheless, it's mostly appropriate when used. For example, once when Thomas was younger, I asked him to straighten his room…

'Thomas, please clean up your room. There are toys and books everywhere.'

'Mom, I think you are obsessed with cleanliness.'

'Really?'

'Yes, in fact – I think we should take you to the doctor. This is not a behavior pattern that I have seen in other mothers. I think you may have some kind of syndrome or something.'

'So you think my behavior pattern (cough, smile, cough) is a sign of a syndrome?'

'Are you mocking me, Mom?'

'In fact I am!'

'Very funny, Mom'

'Hey, I mean it. Clean up your room, Mr.!' I repeated.

'There's that behavior pattern again…'

'Thomas!' I shouted, trying not to smile.

'Okay, okay, sheesh!'

Note: 'Obsessed with cleanliness' he borrowed from a Calvin and Hobbes comic book caption.

Another example…

Thomas' cousin, who was five, absolutely adored him. Although she loved spending time at our house visiting Thomas, his vast collection of books, videos and other valued treasures were equally appealing. Surprisingly, this was okay with Thomas. He enjoyed her company as long as she didn't require a lot of his attention; his preference was to be alone. Once, when she was leaving our home after a particularly long visit, Thomas said his obligatory goodbye to her... once. He figured that's all that was required. She, on the other hand, was known for her lengthy and theatrical farewells.

When Thomas didn't respond to her dramatic and extended goodbye, she threw herself in front of him blowing him kisses, waving, and bellowing her obvious departure. 'Goodbye Thomas, see you next time. Thanks for playing. Thanks for your videos; I'll miss you. Thanks for...' She went on and on. Finally, my sister and I looked at each other and burst out laughing. Noticing our reaction, Thomas stood up, glared at us and said, 'And you wonder why I have issues?'

Note: Later I asked him from where he had borrowed that line. The answer: Timon from *The Lion King 1½*.

Jungle Book story

When Thomas was younger, he loved The *Jungle Book* movie. He watched it over and over and would dance to the blues music that was played throughout the film. Although he didn't always fully articulate his thoughts or speak in full sentences back then, he could sing an entire song perfectly. Once I remember having to bring him with me to a doctor's appointment. He was almost six at the time and was quite content sitting next to me as long as he could read a book. On that particular day, while he quietly read The *Jungle Book*, I noticed him humming to himself as he swung his foot to the beat of his own tune.

When it was my turn to see the doctor, I gently leaned over to Thomas and told him to sit quietly until I returned. I reminded him to check with the lady at the window if he needed anything. Sitting on the other side of Thomas were two ladies in their late sixties. Four other ladies sat around also waiting to be seen. I'd been going to that particular doctor's office for several years, and Thomas had grown to know the office staff quite well. When I motioned to the nurse at front desk that I'd be in with the doctor, she gave me a nod acknowledging Thomas. Not too long after, I heard laughter coming from the waiting room area. I listened more intently as the laughter grew louder. Just as I considered checking on Thomas, a nurse swung open the exam room door and said laughingly, 'Ms Barber, um... your son is quite the little entertainer.'

Not knowing what to expect I hurriedly brushed past her, entering the waiting room area. I saw Thomas standing under the check-in window pretending to be on stage. He was joyfully singing and swaying back and forth, holding his hand in fist as if it were a microphone and belting out a blues tune.

'Shu bee doo doo, I want to walk like you, talk like you,' he sang [humming and dancing]. 'Oh yeah it's truuuuuue sho bee doo doo opp,' [playing an invisible trumpet]. 'Rrrrrrr....mmmm....rrrrrrr......OHHH YEAH!' he sang, happily. As I stood there watching him perform, the elderly ladies watched, laughed and bopped their heads to the beat of his tune. When Thomas finished his song the ladies showed their enthusiasm by clapping. He, in return, smiled and gave them a formal bow.

'Thomas! Thomas,' I called out. When he finally saw me, he smiled but waved me away. I could tell that he was having fun and he didn't want me to interfere. He intimated to the elderly group that he still had one last number to perform. While he sang his last song, I left him to his audience of nurses and patients and returned to the exam room with my doctor.

When it was time to leave the elderly ladies grinned at Thomas shouting, 'Goodbye Thomas, and thank you for your wonderful performance.'

Years later, when I recounted this story to Thomas he laughed remembering the show he put on for the ladies. Then he said to me,

'I wonder how those ladies knew my name when they said goodbye to me.'

'How do you think?' I asked.

'I have no idea. Maybe they guessed,' he said, looking puzzled

'Or, [pause] maybe they heard me call your name,' I said plainly.

'Maybe. Or maybe they just guessed,' he said again.

Calvin & Hobbes and the benefits

When Thomas was about eight, he had a particular interest in comics. On a regular basis he would snatch the Sunday paper and sort through it until he came across the comic section. Soon he became hooked on the *Peanuts* characters, spending hours in the humor section of the local bookstore. Here he also discovered *Calvin & Hobbes* and *Garfield*. If pressed, he would tell you that *Calvin & Hobbes* was 'head and shoulders' above all other comic strips. Many times I would find his nose buried in one of those books and laughing out loud to himself. It didn't matter if he was at home, in the car or at school. The vocabulary in those particular comics was sophisticated and Thomas began to 'borrow' the words he'd read so often and use them in regular conversation. Interestingly, he would also say out loud the words that were meant to be thoughts displayed in the bubbled captions.

Once when I asked him to tidy up his room, for the third time, his response was, 'Sigh...'

'What do you mean 'Sigh'?' I asked him. 'Isn't that something you actually do, not say?'

'It's what Calvin says to Hobbes when he's tired of hearing the same thing over and over again,' he said with a grin.

'Thomas?'

Yawn...' he said, opening his mouth pretending to yawn.

Trying not to smile, I said, 'Pick up your room, Calvin.' In reading comic strips, Thomas was able to closely examine the frame-by-frame pictures. He studied every detail, including the still body language and thoughts of each character. It gave him the opportunity to learn how to anticipate and project what was going to happen next because he could see the exaggerated interaction, and read the thoughts of each character at his own pace. It was a fantastic way to illustrate the connection between comics and nonverbal social cues seen everyday with real people. Surprisingly, he was able to understand and apply the 'borrowed' text and use it in conversations. Once, I couldn't find my car keys and asked Thomas if he would help me find them. He briefly scanned the room, and responded while talking into his wrist (as if it were a small walkie-talkie) saying, 'Houston, we have a problem.'

Lindamood-Bell tutoring

When I realised that Thomas had difficulty generalising concepts, I had him tested through Lindamood-Bell. Lindamood-Bell is an organisation known for their programs which address many learning differences. They use combined methods of teaching including visual, verbal, and auditory strategies. It was an important step toward identifying Thomas' specific needs.

Following the results of an extensive evaluation, Thomas began working with a LMB tutor named Shannon (Thomas called her Shanyon). Shannon was a young, vibrant, and very well trained tutor. She was experienced in working with children who had processing issues. She genuinely enjoyed working with children who learned and understood the world differently.

On Thomas' first day with Shannon I quickly gave her an overview. I explained Thomas' learning style, in which areas I thought his difficulties were, and how he reacted to tasks when he felt he was under pressure. Then I wished her good luck and off I went. Ordinarily, I would have been nervous starting Thomas off with someone new, but this time I wasn't. I saw that Thomas had immediately connected with Shannon, and I felt confident that they would work well together.

Fifty minutes later, I returned and was curious to know how the session had gone. As I stood in the waiting room for Thomas to finish, I realised I could hear their session through the door. I heard Shannon tell Thomas they were just about finished for the day. Then I heard her ask Thomas a question about family. I listened further and heard him say, 'Well, it's like this... my family is cursed. It began generations ago...' The tutor was enthralled.

'Please continue,' she said. Cursed! What did he say? What was he talking about? Then, I heard Thomas continue about how his great, great grandfather was cursed for breaking a promise to a woman many years ago...' Ah! I suddenly recognised the story. He was describing the movie Holes that we'd recently rented and he absolutely loved!

The tutor, of course, didn't know this (right away) and was clearly captured by Thomas' dramatic family story. Again I hear Thomas say, 'Now my family is cursed and...'

'Really, go on,' Shannon replied. I couldn't stand it any longer and I abruptly knocked on the door. Shannon opened the door with a grin. I looked at Thomas and told him that I could hear them through the door while I was waiting. He smiled. I told him how I recognised the story he was sharing about our family and how 'similar' it was to the movie Holes! The tutor burst out laughing, as she too had seen the movie. When I asked Thomas what had prompted him to tell such a story he said, 'Shannon asked me to share an interesting family story. She didn't say what family, so I was portraying Stanley, the main character in the movie Holes. I think he's interesting!'

Graduation celebration

'Oh, we received a graduation invitation,' I announced to Thomas.

'Whose graduation?' he asked.

'Gianna Passalacqua,' I reported. We'd known Gianna since she was born. I couldn't believe she was entering high school.

'Oh, she's graduation from high school?' asked Thomas.

'No, actually, she's graduating from the eighth grade.'

'The eighth grade?' he repeated. 'Mom, everyone knows that you don't graduate from eighth grade. You merely move from the eighth to the ninth grade. It's psychotic! They keep coming up with new ideas to celebrate mediocrity!' Thomas quipped.

Stunned by the sophistication of his remark I asked, 'So what does 'mediocrity' mean Thomas?'

'You know, ordinary or average. In other words – something not needing to be celebrated,' he said with a smirk.

Note: He later told me that the line about mediocrity was borrowed from the movie, The Incredibles.

Inferences

Understanding or making inferences was difficult for Thomas. Whether they were phrases from conversations he'd heard or excerpts from paragraphs he'd read, Thomas had trouble deciphering exactly what was meant if the message was inferred, indirect, implied or somehow circuitous. Although this was something we'd practiced routinely, it was a skill he hadn't yet mastered, and perhaps never would.

For example, on a Saturday afternoon walk, Toni, Thomas' second grade teacher and I talked, walked and laughed for almost an hour before Thomas, who'd been complaining of boredom, decided his legs were 'old' from the exertion. Afterward, and as a consolation, we all stopped to rest and cool off at a local coffee house. That's when we ran into Gina, a friend from the health club. She hadn't met Thomas before, although I'd often talked about him.

'Thomas, this is my friend Gina,' I offered.

'Hi Thomas, it's nice to finally meet you. Your Mom has told me a lot about you,'

Gina said, shaking his hand.

I began chatting and explained that we'd been on a hike when Thomas interrupted me and said, 'Yeah, but I waited in the car for them while they walked.'

'Thomas?' I said, surprised by his remark.

'Well, it was nice to finally meet you Thomas,' Gina said, ignoring his comment and walking away.

As we stood in line to order our drinks, I asked Thomas why he'd said that to Gina. He told me he wanted her to 'realise' he was bored and tired from the walk.

'Bored? Tired? Next time, maybe you should just say, 'I'm bored and tired!'' Noticeably annoyed, I continued, 'What you said gave her a different impression. You didn't imply you were bored. You implied something else!'

'What?' He asked looking confused.

'You implied you were left alone in the car for an hour, Thomas!' I said, shaking my head.

Seconds later, Thomas bolted out the door. Before I could move, Toni dashed after him. Thomas had seen Gina and called out to her across the parking lot. When she came over he nervously explained, 'Um, I wanted to tell you that I actually went on the hike with my Mom, even though I was bored.'

He and Toni promptly returned to the coffee house where he proudly announced that he'd 'implied the correct message'. I told him how nice it was that he took responsibility for the misunderstanding. He was relieved but I, on the other hand, was flabbergasted that he even considered my reaction (perspective) at all, and felt compelled to handle it. Still today, he struggles with how to imply or infer accurately.

Chapter Five

Concrete Thinking

Big Bang theory

Thomas is a concrete thinker and so much of what he believes is based on fact. That's not to say he doesn't believe in fiction or that he doesn't have an imagination. In fact, he is incredibly creative with an elaborate imagination. However, he tends to lean towards the sciences because scientific reasoning, mathematical theories and historical information are based on facts and logic. The information is reliable and dependable and you can account for the results. Many children with AS have difficulty with abstract concepts or unproven theories. It's often easier for them to understand something that is based on fact or can be verified. I know this to be true for Thomas. This is illustrated in a conversation with me about his experience at Bible Camp.

'Thomas, did you like Bible Camp?'

'Kind of!'

'What was the best part of Bible Camp?'

'Art!'

'What was the worst part?'

'The fact that it's based on superstition, not science!'

'How so?'

'There is no physical proof that God actually exists!'

'What do you mean by that?'

'There are just theories... but no proof!'

'Hmm! How do you explain how the world was created?'

'It all started with the Big Bang!'

'Tell me about the Big Bang.'

'The Big Bang is the creation of the Universe according to scientists!'

'Go on...'

'You see, the Universe was created by an explosion, actually a giant ball of gas and fire, throwing tons of dust into the unknown atmosphere. This eventually created a Universe without any edges and no air. Then, a couple of clouds of dust turned into rock and fused together forming the planet known as Earth. Later, air was invented by the forces of nature. That's when life first began in the ocean. All of the earth was covered by ocean then. Eventually, earth evolved into what it is today. Back then it began with strange creatures that came from the sea, then on land, and eventually they evolved into Australipifigus, meaning Southern Ape. Centuries later, apes evolved into humans. Scientists believe that in 15,000 million years from now, there will be something known as The Big Crunch. This will be the end of the Universe as we know it today. Then the process repeats itself with the Big Bang and so on. It's a cycle.'

'So you liked Bible Camp?'

'I guess.'

'Okay, good!'

He watches the Discovery channel.

Note: Although Thomas is not certain of the existence of God, he is quite sure there is a Santa Claus. I am just the writer...

That's not your circle

Thomas dislikes any kind of discord. For him to be calm and productive he requires a harmonious environment. Unfortunately, because life isn't always harmonious, this presents a problem. When he was younger, I realised that the classrooms with the bright lights, loud noise and too many things on the walls were too distracting for him. It was just too much stimuli, but fortunately these things weren't hard to change.

However, because I couldn't predict the behaviour of the outside world I didn't always know what would provoke Thomas into a sensory overload.

For example, when he was about seven, he and I were shopping in a clothing store when we heard a child crying. She was about two, and she would follow her mother around the store whining and carrying on. The mother did not respond to her daughter which only exacerbated the problem for Thomas.

Thomas appeared troubled, so I reassured him that the little girl was probably tired. But when she wouldn't stop crying, like a flash Thomas ran towards the little girl's mother and yelled, 'Excuse me Mrs, but your daughter is crying. Can't you hear her?'

The mother said nothing. I could tell he was getting agitated, so I walked over and took Thomas' hand, slowly moving him away from all the crying and into another department. Quietly, I thanked him for being so concerned about the little girl. But by then Thomas was quite upset. I knew this would escalate and suggested that we leave the store, but not before he yelled across the crowded store, 'Why don't you help your daughter! She's sad! Don't you realise that? What kind of mother are you?'

Finally, Thomas got the attention of the little girl's mother. In fact, he got a lot of attention. We quickly left the store. When we got home and Thomas had calmed down, I explained to him that although it was nice of him to be worried about the little girl, it wasn't his place to say anything to her mother.

This is when I started implementing the phrase, 'That's not your circle.' I had read about a great technique using layers of 'circles' in reference to relationships. This visual example was used to symbolise the relationships of people to the autistic child. With the autistic child in the center, a circle was drawn around that child, with dots representing immediate family members. Then a second circle was drawn around that group to include extended family, teachers and friends. Around that group was another circle with neighbors and church friends. Next was a circle with acquaintances, and then another circle with strangers. Eventually, it looks like a bull's eye. (This technique was descibed by Dr McAfee but was originally created by M.Forest and J.Pearpoint in 1992, see the References list for details.)

I drew this circle for Thomas. When I got to the stranger circle, still expressing my appreciation of his concern for the crying child, I explained to him that in that setting (circle), it would have been more appropriate to say nothing. It wasn't his circle. In the future, I told him I would remind him by simply saying, 'That's not your circle.' I was trying to emphasise what was appropriate conversation and when he should or shouldn't get involved. The goal was eventually to have Thomas recognise for himself what was and wasn't his circle. We continue to use this technique and it has been successful for the most part.

Once, when Thomas was ten, we were in the grocery store standing in the checkout line. It was a crowded Sunday afternoon and the checker was new at her job. Right as we were checking out, I asked the new checker if she would add a box of Presto-Logs to my bill and in my basket. Because she was new, she had to ask a neighboring checker the right code for the logs. When I realised she had brought and charged me for the wrong box of wood, the manager was called. The line grew longer and people were noticeably more impatient. Through all the confusion, the checker became flustered and the manager seemed annoyed with me.

I could tell all of the chaos was starting to upset Thomas. Finally, the new box of wood was brought over and placed into my basket. The manger behaved as if the error was mine and said something to that effect. Noticing all of this was Thomas, who said to the manger, 'Please stop acting like she [pointing to me] imagined all of this. She [again pointing to me] asked for Presto-Logs in the first place. Gosh!'

When the manager walked away, I smiled and thanked everyone for their help. Although I thought it was sweet that Thomas felt the need to defend me, later I told him I didn't think he should have spoken to the manager that way. It was not appropriate.

 'Why, she was in my… I mean in your circle,' he replied.

Flexibility

Flexibility was a word Thomas was very familiar with. Making adjustments to his otherwise rigid way of thinking was something he'd worked on at school and at home. Transitioning to unexpected activities or events had been difficult; still he tried to maintain a flexible attitude.

For as I long as I can remember, Thomas' favorite color had always been blue. When he was about two, he was extremely attached to a plastic blue watering can and he carried it everywhere. After that, it was a tiny blue Little Engine That Could train, followed by a blue pocket size Thomas the Tank Engine. In fact, both were his transition items which were used to reduce meltdowns. A transition item, as we named it, was something important to Thomas that he could carry with him when he transitioned from something. The idea was that it represented something consistent when there was change throughout his day.

I can recall being late for numerous events while trying to find his little blue engine. Finally, I bought four identical blue pocket size Thomas the Tank Engines thinking that if he lost one, I could readily replace it with an identical one. I was wrong. The first time I tried this he knew immediately that it was a different train. How that was possible, I have no idea.

When he was in kindergarten, it was a blue tricycle that he attached himself to. He wouldn't ride the red one, and would tantrum if he couldn't ride the blue one. In first grade he chose a blue camping chair located in the reading corner. Interestingly, the kids in his class seemed to know that Thomas favored the color blue. In fact, his first grade teacher once told me that she witnessed a student saving the blue chair so that when Thomas approached the reading corner, it would be available for him. His teacher quickly remedied that situation by telling Thomas and the other students that he would need to be flexible, and learn to enjoy the colors yellow and green as well.

Once, Thomas lost a baby tooth while playing at the park. He'd put it in his pocket and asked if I'd remind him to put it under his pillow for the tooth fairy that night. Later that day, he realised it was missing and became so upset that I decided to replace it with a tooth he'd lost earlier in the year. I had a collection. Thinking he would be relieved, I appeared with a similar baby tooth and passed it off as the tooth he'd just lost.

He examined the tooth only for a moment before he said, 'Ah Mom, this is not the same tooth!'

'Are you sure?' I asked, surprised he'd even notice the difference.

'Yes, it only resembles the tooth I lost.' He told me.

'Well, do you think it will work, I mean for the tooth fairy?' I asked him.

'No. It's not the correct tooth, but thanks anyway,' he said, and turned on the television. Wow! 'So flexible,' I thought.

A lesson in being flexible

While visiting the Monterey Bay Aquarium, and in an effort to practice math, I gave Thomas a handful of coins for the parking meter. He patiently separated the quarters from the dimes and nickels. He, with my help, calculated how much time we could spend at the aquarium based on the amount of money he put into the meter. This took some time. I saw it as an opportunity to explain how understanding math was important, even in that situation.

As it turned out, there were thirty minutes before closing time by the time we made our way to the aquarium. This, fortunately, didn't upset Thomas as we had season passes and had already planned to return the following day. However, when we returned to our car we found a $20.00 parking ticket stuck to the windshield. I knew right away that it couldn't possibly be correct. By my calculations we should have had an hour and a half left running on the meter. I was livid and Thomas reacted to me by having a complete meltdown.

'I thought we calculated the correct amount of change. We were wrong,' he squealed, wiping the tears from his eyes.

Quickly realising I needed to pull myself together I said, 'Actually, we were not wrong. Something must be wrong with the parking meter or the person handing out the tickets.'

I'd decided, and it was difficult, to shift gears and turn that situation into a lesson. 'We need to be flexible. Let's write a letter to the address on the back of the ticket and explain what happened. We'll tell them that according to our calculations, there should have been a lot more time on the meter, an hour and a half to be exact. In fact, Thomas, they owe us $1.10,' I said.

Together we wrote a letter explaining how we'd carefully figured out how much money was needed to honor the amount of time required to park. Thomas seemed to enjoy this exercise and I thought the example was important. We mailed it to the agency in charge of the meters, and carbon copied the Mayor of Monterey, that was for me. Two weeks later we received two letters. One was from the meter agency apologising for the mistake, and the other was from the Mayor with an enclosed check of $1.10. He said that before he was Mayor, he was a teacher and congratulated Thomas for 'catching' the error.

Adapting

I took Thomas to see *Star Wars Episode III: Revenge of the Sith*. Being a *Star Wars* enthusiast he was thrilled to see it. He'd practically memorised Episodes I, II, IV, V and VI, and was anxious for the details to be revealed in Episode III. Thomas knew that George Lucas had created and directed all of the *Star Wars* films He was someone Thomas admired. He'd studied the trilogy and seemed to understand the new plot. He was able to identify with the characters and tried to explain to me the history of previous episodes so that I would understand the upcoming film. Although I'd been warned that Episode III might be too dark for Thomas, I was relieved when during the film I felt him lean against me whispering what he thought would happen next. He was completely captivated.

In past times, we'd have to leave in the middle of a movie because the acoustics or unanticipated story line was overwhelming for Thomas. Seeing a movie on the big screen in a theater crowded with movie goers was sometimes too much, often initiating a sensory overload. When he was seven, I remember taking him to see the movie *Snow White and the Seven Dwarfs*. He knew the story and I assumed the tale was mild enough. As I often did before a movie began, I reminded him of the happy ending – that Snow White and the Prince lived happily ever after. Whoops, I forgot about the queen and the poisonous apple.

Toward the end of the movie when Snow White fell into a deep sleep because the jealous queen poisoned her, Thomas fell apart. He stood up in the middle of the dark packed movie theater, making his way to the aisle yelling, 'You lied to me. You lied to me.' He stood there wiping his tears but couldn't get it together. I knew what he thought. Even though I told him they lived happily ever after… I didn't say it happened at the end of the movie. I crawled over three people shushing him, whispering loudly 'No, she'll be okay, trust me, it's not over yet.' But he ignored me and ran up the centre aisle and out of the theater. When I finally reached him, he was hysterical. 'You said Snow White lived happily ever after. You didn't say that she died from a bad apple.' When we got home we read the story again and he realised the ending was happy. 'Sorry about that, Mom,' he said calmly.

Four years later, after seeing *Revenge of the Sith*, I told him I was happy to see he'd enjoyed the movie. Then I reminded him of the Snow White experience. He laughed and said, 'Gosh, I am so sorry I overreacted. But you do realise I was a lot younger then.'

Ants

Following a holiday party held at our house, I found the clean up to be too much and chose to leave it for the following day. Bad idea. I'd left a plate of cookies and a bowl full of chocolate covered blueberries out too long. Mounds of ants were now feeding on the leftover treats and I'd already eaten handfuls of the chocolate blueberries. When I realised that the specks were actually families of ants, not to be confused with shaved chocolate, I freaked out. Not only did I have an entire table-top full of ants, I had to have swallowed a couple of dozen.

Later that day, when I relayed the story to Thomas, he was also grossed out on my behalf, or so I thought.

'Oh, Mom, how awful,' he told me, grimacing as if he could imagine my discomfort.

'Isn't that gross?' I said rhetorically.

'Yeah, those poor ants!' he said shaking his head.

'What? What do you mean poor ants? What about me?' I asked, shocked by his take.

'Mom, imagine their death: dark, wet and frightening,' he explained.

'What about me eating all those ants?' I asked again.

'Bugs are protein. Get over it, Mom!'

Note: It's interesting that Thomas instinctively identified with the ants perspective, not mine.

While on vacation

Once, when Thomas was ten, we were on vacation in Arizona and went to the Star Show at the Phoenix Planetarium. This was a real treat for Thomas, as he was extremely interested in the solar system and had become quite knowledgeable. The narrator was a young woman in her mid thirties. She controlled a PowerPoint presentation where specific questions about stars and planets were displayed on a screen and answer buttons were attached to individual chairs in the theater. Thomas was excited to get started. When the narrator began her astronomy presentation, Thomas called out the answers as quickly as the questions appeared. He never missed one and there were thirty questions. He'd memorised the planets and other facts about the solar system in second grade.

And then a surprise... he could barely contain his excitement when he realised that as a bonus feature a slide show called Dragon Planet would be previewed. This show was about prehistoric dinosaurs. Thomas couldn't believe it. Dinosaurs were another passion of his. Again, as we sat there together, Thomas took in every fact and photograph featuring each prehistoric period. He knew more about dinosaurs than most people and at one point in the show, he leaned over and whispered to me that he couldn't believe how lucky he was to see both shows in the same day. As we walked out of the theater after the show, the narrator stopped Thomas and told him how smart she thought he was. He beamed with pride and I was happy to see him feel so good about himself.

Red Ribbon Week

October 25, 2004. It was Red Ribbon Week at the elementary school. Thomas came home from school wearing a red ribbon with 'Say No To Drugs' written down the side of it. Thomas had explained to me that an organisation had visited his classroom discussing the effects of drugs and showed a documentary about high school students who had used tobacco. Their message was simply 'Say No to Drugs'. Thomas told me that throat cancer, tongue cancer and cancer of the jaw were all caused by the use of tobacco. This seemed to have had a great impact on him.

October 29, 2004. It was still Red Ribbon Week. Thomas and I went to the market to pick up a few things we needed for the weekend. As we stood in the check-out line, Thomas noticed that directly across from us was a shelf that housed boxes and boxes of cigarettes and loose tobacco.

'Excuse me, Mr.,' said Thomas, pointing to the tobacco, 'But why are you selling that tobacco?'

The checker looked at the shelf and smirked but didn't respond to Thomas.

Thomas went on, 'Don't you know that tobacco is bad for you? Tobacco will rot your lungs. The nicotine that's inside of the cigarettes will hook on to your lungs and constrict your blood vessels. It may even take your life.'

Still staring at the checker, Thomas said, 'So why are you selling tobacco?'

I couldn't help myself, chiming in with, 'Yeah, so why are you selling tobacco?'

The checker smiled at both of us and said, 'Um, yeah, I don't really know why. I have nothing to do with what the store chooses to sell, sorry.'

'Well, that's too bad,' Thomas told the checker.

We finished checking out and walked towards the car. Thomas was still talking about the terrible effects of tobacco, and again he mentioned the film he'd seen in school. In great detail he described a young man that had to have his jaw removed because of cancer that was caused by tobacco. He was so passionate about his new conviction that I asked him if he wanted to write a letter to the manger of the grocery store explaining his concerns about tobacco.

'No thanks, Mom' he said, crawling into the back seat of our car. 'I don't think my letter will have an impact. All I know is that I will never use tobacco. I will say no to drugs!'

Coincidence or similar interest?

As often as possible, Thomas and I spend time in Capitola, a small beach town in Northern California. One day, we stumbled upon a very cool store in town. The store owner was an older gentleman who was extremely friendly. He immediately saw that Thomas was fascinated by the things in his store and eagerly showed him around, happily pointing out coins, maps, globes, and individual models of the solar system. He was pleased to reveal his assorted supply of dinosaur paraphernalia, in addition to a vast collection of flags. 'He has all fifty states, Mom,' Thomas announced mesmerised by almost everything he saw.

'What a coincidence this is, Mom,' Thomas said, thrilled to uncover such a store.

'What is?' I asked.

'That this store has all the things I'm interested in.'

Interesting or ironic? I wasn't quite sure. I'd scanned the store, surveying the merchandise, and I did agree with Thomas. It was strangely coincidental that so many items would be of interest to Thomas (of great interest). I just didn't say it aloud.

'Mom, can we buy one of the New York State flags for my state report presentation? It's due next week,' Thomas asked.

'Sure,' I said, pleased to know that he was thinking ahead.

'That will be two dollars and fifty cents please,' said the store owner. 'Would you like to buy an 'un-circulated quarter?' he asked Thomas.

'What does that mean?' Thomas inquired.

'Well, it's a quarter that's never been circulated, meaning it's never been in anyone's hand, pocket, or bank,' explained the store owner.

'I guess so,' answered Thomas.

'How much is it?' I asked.

'Um, well it's a quarter,' replied the store owner, looking as though the answer was obvious.

'Oh, I guess that makes sense,' I replied.

As we left the store with the NY state flag and the un-circulated quarter in hand, Thomas said to me, 'I just can't believe that store had so many of my favorite things.'

'Amazing isn't it. It seems like you're not the only person with those same interests,' I told him, glancing back and waving goodbye to the store owner. Interesting indeed!

Solving a mystery with logic

The last week of school, a group of fourth and fifth graders returned from a celebratory end of the year picnic, only to find that their fifth grade classrooms had been toilet papered (TP'd). As a clue, a note was left by the culprits. It read:

Dear Fifth Graders,

Congratulations for completing fifth grade.

Have fun at middle school.

We'll miss you.

Signed, guess who?

'Who did that?' Thomas asked his teacher.

She shrugged in response, claiming not to know. Shortly thereafter, I'd arrived to pick him up, when he immediately directed me into the principal's office.

'Excuse me, Mr. Morre, but will you please sign your name on this piece of paper?' Thomas asked, handing him a blank sheet of paper. 'You see, our classroom was toilet papered and I'm collecting handwriting samples to find the culprit.' The principal willingly offered his signature. Thomas went on to collect and compare signatures from other office personnel, and then returned to his classroom for his teacher to review the evidence.

'Your detective work is incredible, Thomas!' his teacher told him.

It had taken Thomas a while to gather the handwriting samples and so in order not to keep him in further suspense she decided to uncover the mystery for him.

'I actually know who the culprits are,' she whispered.

'Who are they?' Thomas excitedly asked.

'The third grade teachers,' she let slip. 'I know this because our grade has toilet papered them in the past. It's done in fun,' she explained, making sure he understood it was not mean spirited.

'Then I guess there's no real mystery here,' Thomas replied, handing her the list of writing samples. 'My work here is finished!'

Parallel

Driving home from school one day, Thomas sat in the back reviewing his flash cards for a geometry quiz the next day. He explained that one side of the card was a diagram of a geometric shape, while the other side named that shape. As I drove along, I asked him to name and describe each shape to me. I thought it was a great way for him to study for his quiz. I couldn't see the flashcards so I tried to guess the shape based on his clues. After he'd described several geometric shapes, he got to the word parallel. 'Parallel,' he announced. Before he could describe it, I quickly chimed in with, 'Parallel… the number eleven.'

'What are you talking about, Mom?' Thomas argued.

'Parallel,' I repeated. 'It looks like the number eleven, don't you think?' I said.

'No, I don't,' he said, then paused.

'Parallel,' he repeated. 'An equal sign lying on its side,' he said, correcting me.

'What's wrong with saying parallel looks like the number eleven?' I questioned.

'Nothing. Except that it's not accurate. The number eleven is actually two number ones standing next to each other,' he said confidently. Then he asked if he could finish studying without my help.

Outrageous animal facts

On a road trip, Thomas and I decided to pass the time by trying to name the most outrageous animal facts. It's a game we'd play to sharpen our skills, my skills actually. Facts are easy for Thomas to retain, and so his focus was on the turn-taking part of the game.

'You go first, Mom,' said Thomas.

'Okay, did you know that caterpillars evolve into butterflies?' I asked.

'Yes, since kindergarten. Okay, did you know clams can change their sex?' he asked.

'Really?' I said, surprised by that fact.

'Yes, really, but only once. All clams are actually born male,' Thomas asserted.

'Interesting! Okay, did you know that red ants are the most creative ants on the planet?' I quipped.

Realising I made that one up, Thomas dramatically rolled his eyes and said, 'Okay, did you know that a cockroach can live for eight days without his head?'

He was pretty confident I wouldn't be able to top that fact.

'Are you sure? That's hard to believe,' I asked (who knew that?).

'Yes, their brains are in their bodies. They only end up dying because they need food,' Thomas replied with absolute certainty.

'Okay, top this – did you know that house flies have eyelashes?'

'Actually, no insect has eyelashes,' he said, shaking his head.

'Did you know whales used to have legs?' Thomas reported, certain that he'd topped me.

'Wow! Okay, top this one – did you know that snakes can detect the presence of humans through their sensory impulses?' I said, thinking it sounded outrageous and logical.

'You mean heat seeker pits, don't you?' Thomas said, correcting me.

'Okay… I'm pretty sure you won, Thomas!'

Chapter Six

Perspective Taking

Perspective taking in a restaurant

Children with AS often have difficulty understanding someone else's perspective. Consequently, they tend to focus on their own point of view, often assuming 'you know what they know'. As a result, social responses to questions or comments are frequently made inappropriately and are often misunderstood. This can be frustrating for an AS child, as it interferes with his attempt to be social and interact with others.

Realising that this was an issue for Thomas I made a conscious effort to practice appropriate social interaction and invited him to dine with me at a fancy restaurant. A linen tablecloth and more than one fork constitute a fancy restaurant. I considered a restaurant to be a structured and fairly predictable setting where Thomas could try appropriate social interaction. Thomas and I arrived at the restaurant, checked in and were quickly seated. Thomas attempted to order off the menu independently while the waiter patiently awaited his selection. Note: Thomas was on a gluten free casein free diet.

'I'll have a plain hamburger, no bun, no seasoning, with plain french fries, and a glass of ice water with one straw… please,' Thomas said politely.

'How would you like your hamburger cooked, sir?' asked the waiter.

'Completely,' Thomas replied.

'Would you like cheese on your burger, sir?' the waiter inquired.

'No! Don't you realise I can't have wheat or dairy?' Thomas screamed to the waiter.

Of course, now we had the attention of everyone in the entire restaurant. The waiter stood by our table for a moment looking surprised, and then walked away.

I quietly asked Thomas, 'Have you ever met that waiter before?'

'No,' he replied.

I waited a moment and then asked him, 'If you've never met the waiter before, then how could he know that you can't have wheat or dairy?'

'I don't know!' Thomas answered.

'Well, if I haven't told him about your diet, and you haven't told him about your diet, how would he know about your diet?' I asked him.

'I guess he would have no idea. I never realised,' he said.

The waiter returned to our table and stood patiently while Thomas apologised for his tone of voice. Then Thomas repeated his order to the waiter.

'I'll have a plain hamburger – hold the bun – plain french fries – hold the seasoning, with a glass of ice water, and a straw… please.' Thomas continued, 'I am on a special diet. I don't eat wheat or dairy.'

The waiter walked away and cautiously returned with Thomas' exact order. Thomas thanked the waiter appropriately.

We frequent that particular restaurant to practice ordering and interacting. The staff has grown to understand Thomas and welcomes our visits. No one has asked Thomas if he would like cheese on his burger since our first visit. They simply ask him if he would like anything else with his order.

In that setting, I purposely chose to discuss with Thomas the reason the waiter couldn't have known he was on a special diet, and why. By addressing that particular issue instead of the way he responded to the waiter, which appeared to be rude, it gave Thomas the opportunity to realise the waiter's perspective versus his own.

Perspective taking – communicating or lack thereof…

Communicating was difficult for Thomas at times, so he processed information differently and his expressive and receptive language delays only complicated his ability to convey his thoughts and share information. This rigid way of thinking, especially when he was younger, often makes it hard for him accept things. As a result meltdowns were a common occurrence.

Once, when Thomas was about six, we were standing outside a shopping mall together when he asked if we could go to the bookstore. I told him that we couldn't. It had been a long day and I told him it was time to go home. Often he would get so upset that he would go from zero to ten and fire me as his mother. As I attempted to get him to walk towards the car, he angrily started screaming, 'You're not my mother. Leave me alone.' Although I tried to ignore him, he continued yelling, 'You're not my mother.'

Pretty soon, an older gentleman walked over towards us. While Thomas continued to melt down, the man interrupted us and said, 'Excuse me Ms, but, is there a problem?'

I thought the problem was obvious. My son was trying to wrestle himself away from me as I tried to move him toward the parking lot.

'No, well not really. My son is just having a hard time,' I replied.

'You're not my mother,' Thomas yelled again.

I was embarrassed. I stood quietly and stared at Thomas. The next thing you know, the man was glaring at me. Suddenly, he leaned toward me and sharply questioned, 'Well, are you his mother?'

I said nothing.

'Well are you?' The man repeated.

'Yes, in fact I am,' I said to him, clearly annoyed.

The man turned to Thomas and asked, 'Is this your mother?' He was obviously not convinced.

I stood there, with my mouth open and rolled my eyes.

'Oh, brother!' I finally screeched, staring right into the man's face.

'Thomas, tell the man I am your mother!' I demanded.

He said nothing. He was mad at me.

The man looked at me. I looked at the man. Thomas avoided looking at both of us.

Finally Thomas announced, 'Yes, she's my mother.' [Pausing] 'Why do you ask?'

'Why what?' said the man. Now he was annoyed.

'Why did you ask me if she's my mother?' Thomas asked the man again.

I raised my eyebrows and smiled at the man, but the man didn't respond to me or to Thomas. He just shook his head and walked away. I am sure he thought Thomas was joking with him.

'Can we go home now, Mom?' Thomas asked.

'Yes!' I told him.

Things aren't always as they appear. I remember once when Thomas was about five, he and I were standing in line for the ladies public restroom at the local playhouse. It was during the intermission for the Christmas Play, The

Scrooge. As we approached the entrance for the restroom, a woman remarked about why I shouldn't bring my little boy into a restroom for ladies. I briefly commented that it was better if he was with me.

Apparently, she didn't understand because she continued to disagree, loudly. I remained in line and continued to ignore her. She told me that she wanted him to leave. Thomas started to get nervous and wanted to know why the lady was so upset. Because Asperger's isn't an obvious disability, the woman could not understand the assistance he required.

Finally, I smiled at the woman, choosing not to be affected (which was difficult) and simply said, 'Let's just assume you don't understand the circumstances.' With that, I pointed Thomas into the ladies bathroom stall while I waited. The woman remained quiet. When Thomas finished, he washed his hands and waved goodbye to the woman. As we returned to our seats in the theater, so did the woman. Coincidentally, she was sitting right behind us. Thomas and I enjoyed the rest of the play.

Motivated by math

Thomas hated math. He claimed he had 'math-block' and viewed it as a deficit. From a very young age, Thomas realised that he excelled academically and was stunned to discover that his abilities and expertise didn't automatically spill over to every area, including math.

Mrs D, Thomas' 5th grade teacher, developed a reward system that allowed all her students to earn D-Dollars. These dollars could be earned and used a number of ways. Helping, caring, and sharing with fellow classmates were the big dollar earners. A wall chart described which behavior and good deeds warranted which rewards. At the top of that list was home-work buy-back. Meaning: if enough D-Dollars were earned, students could buy back complete sections of their daily homework. Thomas thought any opportunity that would get him out of math was wonderful.

After school one day, Thomas ran out of his classroom and excitedly announced that he had no math homework for the evening. He said he'd earned and saved enough D-Dollars to buy back his math homework. I glanced over to his teacher who nodded to me, confirming his excitement.

'Wow, much did that cost you?' I asked.

'25 big ones,' he quipped. He said it was well worth it because they had three pages of math. 'Three, Mom!'

Interestingly, eliminating math homework was Thomas' motivation to 'think about' his fellow classmates. What a great idea!

A social conscience

It's sometimes difficult for Thomas to determine what information is relevant and what isn't. Most people can take information and either store it and use it later, or apply it appropriately to a current conversation or situation. For someone with AS, it's often hard to decipher what's pertinent or how to tie it together. And then again, at times it's not that difficult. For example, mid year in fifth grade, Thomas came home with his homework assignment. He was to complete the rough draft of a persuasive essay that he'd started at school. When I read it, I realised he'd combined the movie making industry, his passion, with strategies of how it could solve the California budget crisis (his words). He worked on it unassisted and turned it in the following day.

The next morning, I saw his teacher in the office. I asked her about the assignment, which I thought was quite sophisticated for a class of fifth graders.

'What assignment?' she asked, puzzled.

'The essay,' I told her.

'You mean, the Persuasive Essay?' she asked.

'Yes,' I answered back, still thinking that the budget crisis was a pretty complex topic.

'Oh, what did Thomas write about? I haven't looked at it yet,' she said curiously.

'Movie making and the budget crisis.'

'Budget crisis?' she repeated, as if she were surprised by the topic.

'Yes... the budget crisis,' I repeated. 'You must have been discussing it in class!'

'Ah... no!' she said with a chuckle.

I proceeded to tell her what Thomas had written and she, along with the entire office staff, couldn't believe their ears. The same child who is supposed to have difficulty with perspective taking is the child with a social conscience.

The essay…

March 10, 2005

Persuasive Essay

Everyone enjoys the movies. Movie makers make life a little bit 'cooler' for Americans. Making movies is a form of creativity and a way to make money. We can help the California budget crisis by going to the movies.

The movie industry has a lot of money. Perhaps movie makers or movie theater owners in California could charge a little extra per movie ticket.

It's true that no one likes to be told what to do. For example, when the British told the colonists they had to pay extra tax for tea and stuff, the colonists didn't like it.

So, Californians could decide if they would like to donate any extra money at all. If they do, they could give one or two percent extra for each movie ticket they bought. It could work like this: for example, a red ticket means the movie ticket costs 1% more than the usual ticket. A blue ticket would cost 2% more. [At that time, Thomas' class was studying the American Revolution, Red coats versus the Blue coats. Hence, the color he chose for the tickets and his reference to the tax on tea.]

The extra money could be sent to the Governor. He used to be a movie star. If we all work together, we could collect enough money to fix our budget for schools. I think going to the movies can save our schools and fix our budget crisis!

Curious, I later asked Thomas where he had heard about the budget crisis.

'From you, Mom,' He told me.

'Me? When?' I questioned.

'Yes. Remember last week when you helped me find a political cartoon for another assignment?' he asked.

'Yes!'

'Well, that's when you told me about the budget crisis. You see, there was a cartoon with a man standing in front of a group of people, and the caption over his head read, 'These experts are here to help solve the budget crisis.' And then the man pointed to three experts sitting behind a table. [He begins laughing hysterically.] One was the tooth fairy, one was the Easter Bunny and one was Pinocchio. I didn't understand the cartoon. So, you explained what the budget crisis was and how the tooth fairy, Easter Bunny and Pinocchio couldn't possibly solve the budget crisis. Then I got it,' he explained.

'Oh my goodness, Thomas!' I couldn't believe it.

'So, since I had to write a persuasive essay, I thought I would persuade other kids to help fix the budget crisis with movies, my favorite thing,' he told me.

'You are kind and brilliant!' I announced.

Note to reader: I sent his essay to the Governor of California (and The First Lady) and he responded two weeks later, thanking Thomas for his interest. When Thomas read his reply, he said to me, 'Mom, he didn't mention if he was going to use my idea.'

Growing up

On our way to Stanford University for a fundraising function, I explained to Thomas that Stanford was a prestigious college. 'Maybe you can be a student there one day?' I offered.

'How far is it from our home?' Thomas asked.

'Only an hour.'

'Well, would I have to live there if I went to college there?'

'It depends. If you did, it might be easier because you wouldn't have to commute back and forth from our house for classes,' I explained.

'Well, if I do decide to go to Stanford, I'll move back to our town when I finish college,' he assured me.

'Okay. When that happens, I'll move out so that you can live in our house,' I offered.

'Why would you move out?' he asked.

'Who knows, maybe by that time I'll want to retire and move away.'

'Well, don't move too far away. My kids will want to visit you a lot!' Thomas informed me.

'Okay,' I said smiling, happy to know he was thinking about his future.

After a noticeable silence Thomas said, 'You know Mom; I'm thinking maybe you shouldn't move away at all. You'll need to take care of my kids after school while I'm at work.'

'Maybe your wife will take care of your kids when you're at work!' 'Wife! I'm not going to have a wife!' Thomas exclaimed.

'Oh… I just thought…'

'I'm going to adopt all my kids!' Thomas proclaimed.

Okay then,' I said, smiling.

Having Empathy

When Thomas was seven, Gracie passed away. She was ninety six and his great, great grandmother. We'd spent many afternoons visiting her at the assisted living home, not far from where we lived. During the last year of her life she grew more disoriented, occasionally confusing her past with the present. Eventually, Gracie had difficultly expressing her thoughts or needs, and Thomas was acutely aware of this.

I remember one particular visit well; while Gracie reminisced about a train ride she'd taken as a young girl, she became extremely frustrated when she couldn't quite remember the details. While my sister and I tried to decipher her story, Thomas grew noticeably upset. 'She's trying to tell you about a train ride she took long ago. Now she thinks it happened yesterday, just let her speak. She knows she's confused, that's why she's mad,' he screamed. I looked at my sister in utter amazement. To my surprise, he understood it all.

Not long after that, Gracie passed away. I remember explaining to Thomas how sad we were to lose her, especially my mother, Kitty-Gram. I wanted him to realise her grief and asked him to be especially sensitive. That evening, I remember him walking right up to my mother offering, 'Kitty-gram, I have a great idea. Maybe we can make Gracie's birthday a holiday in our family.

Then you could celebrate that day every year.' My mother started to cry and Thomas looked confused.

'What a great idea,' she told him through tears.

* * *

Four years later Thomas' uncle Marc died of colon cancer, devastating our entire family. He was only forty-one and Thomas adored him. Thomas had great difficulty dealing with this loss. For days, he carried around a photograph of himself with his Uncle Marc. When he chose not to attend Marc's funeral, I had concerns about him understanding the finality of it all. Months later, we visited the cemetery where Marc was placed to rest. Thomas informed me that he preferred never to return. When I asked him why he said, 'He's gone. He's not here (pointing to the head stone). He's probably hanging out with Zeus, the King of the Gods. There's no need to worship his headstone.'

'Zeus?' I repeated.

'You never know,' he replied, feeling comforted by his own imagination.

Chapter Seven

The Literal Child

Curious Thomas

Thomas was, and still is, a huge fan of Lego models. He would build elaborate and complicated structures without looking at the directions in record time and with absolute ease. I noticed that, from an early age, he was interested in order. He seemed to be curious about the cause and effect of things and spent a lot of time trying to figure out what he could fit together. Once, when a friend and I were playing a game of Cribbage, Thomas (almost two years old at the time), approached the Cribbage board and removed all the colored pegs that were scattered strategically on the board. I watched while he replaced each peg in a color coordinated order. I was curious by his interest in order and was intrigued by his ability to organise. That's when I first discovered he recognised color differences.

I enjoyed watching him crawl. When he was about two, he would crawl under the dining room table and purposely, but gently, bump his head and then measure with his hands the distance between the table and his head. He would do this over and over, as if wanting to understand the cause and effect of his action.

Note: When Thomas was older I reminded him of this story. Although he thought it was hysterically funny, he couldn't recall it.

Thomas loved to make things out of blank white paper and sticky tape. He would make intricate airplanes, sophisticated trains, and complex buildings with many parts and shapes. What was interesting was that he never first drew what he cut out, he'd just start cutting. This was amazing to me. He'd instinctively know what size and shape each piece had to be to proportionately fit his design. He'd cut them precisely and accurately every time. He had great visual perceptual awareness.

Thomas and sticky tape go way back. At his fifth birthday party, a helium balloon got loose and floated to the top of the vaulted ceiling in our house. I promised I would get it down for him after the party, as it was high and stuck in a hard to reach corner. But he couldn't wait. After he'd blown out his birthday candles he immediately dragged a chair across the room and placed it right under the balloon. Saying nothing to me, he handed me an umbrella while he rolled a piece of sticky tape around the very tip of it. He made it clear that he wanted me to reach up and touch the balloon with the tip of the umbrella. I told him I didn't know if the sticky tape would be sticky enough to grasp the balloon and pull it down, but I would try. When I reached up to get it, to my surprise, it stuck to the balloon. It came right down and I handed it to Thomas. He was happy. I was amazed.

Honesty

Children with AS, I have discovered, can be brutally honest. They can't help it. They simply don't know any other way to be. They are generally high-principled children with a clear sense of what's right and what's wrong. Therefore, they usually don't mince words and they often speak without editing their thoughts. They'll tell you exactly what they're thinking and more often than not, it's unsolicited. Sometimes they may offer comments that are personal or harsh. Other times, they'll share advice or information that has no relevance to the listener.

For example, once Thomas' elementary school principal introduced him to a gentleman teacher who was visiting the school campus. Thomas said hello, shook his hand and then said to the man, 'You are very tall and appear to be quite bald.' The man smiled and touched the top of his head. Then, the man answered back, 'Why yes, I am tall, and I'd say a bit bald. It is very nice to meet you Thomas.' Later, when the principal told me the story, I asked if the gentleman teacher had been offended by Thomas' comments. Thankfully, he wasn't.

Another time, Thomas stopped one of the first grade teachers to ask her the time. When she leaned down close to him to answer his question, he interrupted her and announced, 'I never realised before that you had so many wrinkles around your eyes.' Then he went on to question her if they were new wrinkles, stating he'd never noticed them before. I'd arrived at the end of that conversation, catching only the last affront and quickly offered her a compliment, which he promptly repeated. Luckily, she was a teacher who'd known Thomas well and was amused by his remarks.

Unfortunately, his comments were not always so well received. When Thomas was about six, he saw a woman in the post office that was very overweight. After staring at her for several minutes, Thomas walked right up to her and said, 'I've noticed that you are quite large.' She, of course, thought he was quite rude. She scowled at him, while mumbling to herself something about how he should be punished for his bad manners. I quickly called to Thomas, awkwardly apologised to the woman and then whisked him into the car.

Afterward, I asked him, 'Did you notice the woman's facial expression when you so bluntly pointed out her large size?'

'I didn't,' he said.

'By stating to the woman that she was quite large, do you think you could have hurt her feelings?' I asked him.

'No, why do you ask?' he said.

After a moment of silence, I realised that nothing I was saying was making any sense to him. Then he asked me if I thought the woman was large. I told him I did. He asked if I thought she thought that she was large. I told him I thought she did.

'Then what's the mystery?' he asked.

I explained to him that she probably wouldn't want him or anyone else to point it out to her. He wanted to know why. I told him I thought she might be sensitive about her size. He asked what 'sensitive' looked like on someone's face. I didn't know what to say. Then I reminded him how she'd scowled at him earlier. He claimed a scowl, which he missed, was a scowl and wanted to know what it had to do with anything we were talking about.

This went on for about thirty minutes. Finally, I decided that the new rule was that he wouldn't remark to anyone about their size, height, weight, race, wrinkles or bald head. Thomas agreed to the new rule, even though he didn't really understand it. It was difficult for him to read, understand or follow the unspoken social cues that are present in everyday interaction. Communicating appropriately was something he practiced regularly, but learned incrementally.

Telling more truth

As my face began to heal from the removal of a cancer growth on the side of my nose, I noticed my skin retracting, as promised by the doctor, in such a way that it actually changed the shape of my left nostril. While happy to know all the skin cancer was gone, I was left with a misshapen and uneven nose. About three weeks after the procedure, Thomas and I were riding along in the car (we're in our car a lot). While stopped at a traffic light I turned around and asked him if he'd noticed anything different about my nose.

'What do you mean, different?' He asked.

'Well, do you think my nostrils are the same shape after the surgery?' I asked him. I knew he would tell me the truth.

'I need a more informative view!' he announced.

'Meaning what exactly?' I asked him.

'Mom, look into the mirror (the rear-view mirror) and look up like this,' he said. Then he held his head back and looked up to model the position for me.

As I held my head back while still looking in the mirror, he peered behind me in the mirror to get a better look. I started to laugh when he said in a serious voice, 'Well, they're both the same shape. It's just that one nostril happens to be a bit smaller than the other one. I'm afraid it's the left one!'

'What? Really?' I said. It was obvious to him that I was bothered by his observation.

'It's not very noticeable – unless of course, someone looked up your nose.' He was trying to make me feel better.

Then he said, 'Mom, actually I think you look like Rapunzel, but with shorter hair.'

'What does that mean?' I asked, confused.

'Nothing, I was just trying to distract you like you do to me when I'm upset about something. Did it work?' he asked, totally aware of my diversion tactic.

'Yes. Thanks!' I told him.

Say what you mean and mean what you say

I learned early on to say what I mean and mean what I say when talking to Thomas. He, like other AS children, tends to be very literal. Once in second grade, his class assignment was to give an oral presentation about his heritage. Because he's of Irish decent, his report was on the potato famine. I remember he was very interested in the facts surrounding that period of time. He spent many hours on the internet and had his nose in books researching the history of that period. Together we worked on his report until he was comfortable with his oral presentation. We rehearsed his speech about the potato famine only once. He informed me that the report did not require practice, as it was simply a report based on fact. I trusted his judgment but did offer one piece of advice. I assumed he would be nervous about his first public speaking attempt, so I told him to pretend to be an actor in a play instead of a student giving a presentation.

On the morning of his presentation, I arrived early to the classroom and sat in the back. Apparently several other parents had already come and gone and even video taped their children's presentations. As Thomas stood and prepared to present his report, I remember feeling extremely proud. I knew that he had worked hard and was sure he would do a great job presenting the facts. When it was his turn, he stood and introduced himself and he began with the facts describing that period. Following his first fact about how many people had died during that period, a little boy immediately raised his hand. 'How many people lived during that time?' he asked Thomas.

'I don't know the exact number of how many people lived. But I do know my ancestors lived,' Thomas quickly replied.

'How do you know that?' asked the child.

'Because if they had died, I wouldn't be here today giving this report,' he answered matter of factly.

Shortly thereafter, he interrupted himself and pretended to take a phone call. He pretended to hold a telephone in his hand while he spoke into the receiver. He told the caller that he couldn't talk right then, as he was in the middle of giving an important presentation. I quickly told his aide to whisper in his ear for him not take any more phone calls until after his presentation. The teacher and students thought it was hilarious, and I of course realised he had taken my advice. After he finished his report (which was given huge applause) I asked him about the telephone call he'd received. As I predicted, he said he was just acting a part, just like I told him to.

'Well, you were fabulous,' I said proudly.

Say what you mean and mean what you say I told myself!

**

Once when Thomas was little, I was reading to him at bedtime. When the story was over, he turned the light out and threw the book on the floor. I said to him, 'Do you think you might trip on the book if you get up during the night?'

He said, 'Nope, I know where it is on the floor.' I waited a moment, but still wanted to make my point.

'Well, if I were to get up in the middle of the night, do you think I might step on that book?' I asked.

He quickly sat up, turned on the light, hopped off the bed from the side I was on and said, 'Um, pretend I'm your size.' He then walked around the bed and carefully stepped over the book and turned to me and said, 'Nope, not if you're careful!'

This last summer, Thomas' bible camp leader called to talk to Thomas. The camp does this every year as part of their program to establish a connection with each child prior to the start of camp. Thomas had attended this particular camp twice before and enjoyed the experience. I answered the telephone and she introduced herself as Thomas' camp leader and asked to speak to him. 'Thomas, hey Tom,' I called out to him from across the house. I waited a few minutes for him to respond. Finally he came to the phone.

After hearing me address him as both Thomas and Tom, I could tell she asked him which name he preferred. He replied, 'Um, you can call me Ben.' I started to laugh, and thought to myself, why would he rename himself? I could tell she asked him if Ben was his middle name. 'No, my middle name is Joseph,' he told her. When they finished talking, I got back on the telephone and by that time, she was laughing too. I clarified for her that Thomas went by the name Thomas and that I didn't know why he picked the name Ben. She laughed again. She 'gets it'. I hung up the telephone and asked Thomas why he wanted to be called Ben. He told me that the counselor had asked him what name he would like to be called. He told her Ben because it was a name he liked.

* * *

Once, when Thomas was in fourth grade he went to the train museum on a class field trip with his school. Thomas loved trains. Until he was about five, trains were an area of great interest, a focus for him. He was quite an expert on the various types, where they traveled and other information. Thus I knew that particular field trip would be a great time for him. I also knew he might be easily distracted and was concerned he might separate himself from the group. I cautioned him to stay with his classmates even if he was curious about something they weren't studying. I told him to call my cellular phone if he got lost from the group. About half way into the field trip Thomas and his aide wandered off to investigate a train that Thomas had been interested in. When the aide noticed she lost sight of their group she announced to Thomas, 'We appear to be lost so we'd better start looking for our class now.' Thomas replied, 'I need to find a pay phone.' 'Why?' his aide inquired. Thomas continued with, 'My mom told me that if I got lost on this field trip I was supposed to call her cell phone immediately. So, I need to find a pay phone.' His aide put her arm around his shoulder and kindly assured him that he wasn't technically lost if he was with her.

Another time, Thomas and I went to see a friend perform in the play Peter Pan. Thomas loved the arts and we were season ticket holders to the local playhouse in town. It was also a great opportunity to expose him, in a social sense, to the live and on stage exaggerated expressions of communication through art. Although Thomas missed subtle nuances of nonverbal communication, he did get the obvious interaction of characters in a play.

At one point in the play, the narrator involved the audience by asking them to clap their hands if they could see Tinkerbell's light. All clapped but Thomas. Then the narrator asked the audience to clap if they saw Tinkerbell's light fading. All clapped but Thomas. Then the narrator advised the audience that if they believed in fairies they should clap loud enough for Tinkerbell to shine bright again. All clapped but Thomas. Noticing this, a friend leaned over and asked Thomas why he never clapped for Tinker Bell. His reply was simple and literal. He said, 'The fairy that the narrator referred to as Tinkerbell was actually a reflection of a pen light, not a fairy.' And then he pointed to the man still holding the pen light on the side of the stage. True. The narrator never said to clap if you believe in pen lights.

* * *

Many teachers that had Thomas in their classes went beyond the call of duty to involve him with his peers while assisting him in academic areas. Thomas' aide would report daily about Thomas and the events of the day. Once in second grade, Thomas' teacher, realising math was a difficult subject for him, asked him if he'd be her assistant in front of the class. She'd been solving a math problem and thought she could involve him by eliciting his help. He agreed. He stood next to her as she worked from the overhead projector. In fact, he continued to stand next to her as requested, with no idea he should return to his seat after solving the math problem. The teacher noticed that he was soon mimicking her movements, also realising that when she'd asked for his help, she hadn't said for how long. Patiently, she waited until the recess bell rang before thanking him. She also informed him that she'd be carrying on the rest of the day without him.

Phoebe syndrome

One of my friends is a well-known author of children's books. When I realised her latest book would be available at our local bookstore, I quickly went out and bought it for Thomas. It was called, My Mom and Other Mysteries of the Universe. It was full of sarcasm and inferences, and I thought it would be great practice for Thomas. After school that day, I told him that I had a surprise for him and handed him the book. He absolutely loved to read books.

'Wow, Mom. Thanks!' Thomas said happily.

'And guess what else?' I said.

'What else?' he repeated.

'I know the author of that book,' I announced proudly, pointing to the book.

'Who is the author?' he asked me, while at the same time reading her name aloud off the cover. When he was younger he loved going to bookstores when the authors themselves were there to read and sign their books.

'She is a friend of mine. We exercise together in the mornings after I drop you off for school,' I told him. I'm sure it never occurred to him that I have a life after I drop him off for school.

'Wow, what a coincidence!' he said, as if he were genuinely surprised.

'What's a coincidence?' I repeated.

'That you actually bought this book for me and you happen to know the author too,' he said. It didn't compute for him so I explained.

'Oh! Well, I actually knew in advance that my friend was the author of the book. That's why I bought you the book!' I told him, trying to be clearer.

'Oh! Cool!' he said happily, but I don't know if he really understood the connection.

* * *

Another time, when Thomas was eleven, I was replacing the counter top in our kitchen and wanted his opinion on the new selection of replacement tile. As I placed three different tiles out on the counter, I asked him, 'Which one catches your eye?' As soon as I said the sentence, I knew I should have rephrased it.

He immediately walked over to the counter, stood sideways facing the other direction, and looked at the tiles from only the corner of his eye.

'What are you doing?' I asked.

'I'm standing here to see if one of them will catch my eye,' he told me ever so seriously. Then he announced, 'Unfortunately, none of them do. Mom, you'll have to decide for yourself.' And with that, he walked away.

* * *

Once, when Thomas and I arrived early for an appointment, we'd decided to park in the lot in a shaded area, spending the extra time catching up on reading. While we waited, Thomas began to rhythmically tap his fingers on the side door panel, over and over and over. Normally this would not have bothered me, but as the sound grew louder, I turned around and patiently (but firmly) asked him to stop tapping his fingers.

'These fingers?' he asked, wiggling the fingers on his right hand.

'Yes, those fingers,' I told him.

Pretty soon, I heard the tapping begin again. I waited for several minutes before I turned around shouting his name, clearly annoyed that he'd ignored my earlier request. He was looking out the window, but still tapping his fingers on his left hand. Again, I said his name aloud.

When I finally got his attention, he noticed that I was silent but staring at his left hand. He immediately looked up and said to me, 'By the look on your face, I'm guessing you don't want me to tap the fingers on this hand either right?'

Note: I was shocked to know he was 'reading' my face. Sometimes Thomas reminds me of the character Phoebe, on the show Friends.

Hanukkah…

It was the second week of December when Thomas asked me, 'Mom, do you realise that tomorrow is the first day of Hanukkah?'

'In fact I do know that,' I told him.

The following evening as we were leaving Thomas' weekly social skills group, he abruptly stopped and turned to me in front of the teacher and five mothers and their children. He said, 'Mom, tonight is the first night of Hanukkah. Do you have my Hanukkah gift?'

Several parents stopped and looked at me but I chose not to answer his question. Instead, I hurriedly moved him towards the door. Again, Thomas repeated (but this time much louder), 'Mom, tonight is the first night of Hanukkah. Do you have my Hanukkah gift?'

Suddenly, the room fell quiet and all the parents and his teacher just stood looking at me waiting for my response. Realising then that I needed to answer Thomas, I quietly leaned over to him and whispered into his ear, 'Honey, I do know it's the first day of Hanukkah… but we are not Jewish.'

'So, what does that have to do with celebrating Hanukkah?' he yelled out.

Just then, I looked over at the other parents in the room and announced, 'Yeah, um… we're pretty much not Jewish.' All of them burst out laughing. They thought the exchange between us was absolutely hilarious.

When I finally got Thomas in the car, he told me that his class at school had been discussing different religions and how they'd celebrated their religious holidays. I asked him what made him think he was supposed to celebrate a Jewish holiday when he was not Jewish. His reply was, 'Well, why limit yourself?'

Walk through the American Revolution

As part of Thomas' social studies unit, his fifth grade teacher arranged to have a 'walk through the revolution,' as an adjunct to the material already covered in class. This 'walk' depicted the facts and history of the American Revolution. Students portrayed many of the great heroes of that period, while a number of historical events were dramatically reenacted. Thomas chose Benjamin Franklin. Thomas' balding appearance, brown knickers and square glasses were clever, but nothing topped his theatrical portrayal of Benjamin Franklin. As the oldest signer of the Declaration of Independence, Thomas delivered his interpretation of Benjamin Franklin and recounted many of his achievements.

I was in the audience that day when I overheard the skit coordinator explain to the students how they could earn points for their red, white and blue coat teaMs She told them she would give points to those students who 'looked respectful' to their fellow classmates. During the event, she periodically selected respectful children and added points to their teaMs The team with the most points at the end of the skit was considered the winning team.

At one point, Thomas turned to me and whispered, 'Mom, what does respectful look like? I want to be 'noticed' for being respectful too.' His aide and I smiled at each other while I whispered back, 'Looking respectful requires looking at the student speaker and quietly listening to them while they give their presentation.'

Thomas sat in his seat trying to look respectful. After a while, he quietly raised his hand. When the coordinator called on Thomas, he stood up, cuffed his hand to his mouth, cleared his throat and whispered, 'Could you please notice me being respectful?'

State report conversation

Generalising information was extremely difficult for Thomas. In the past, he was unable to do this effectively because he had trouble with discerning relevant information. He struggled with knowing what information was applicable to a given situation. This was an issue for him, so at home we read passages from books or magazine articles and then Thomas would paraphrase the information. The strategy seemed to be effective. Since this was a critical skill to be missing, Thomas worked on generalising specific information in various contexts with his LindamoodBell tutor twice a week.

In fifth grade, one of his biggest assignments of the year was writing a state report. Thomas chose the state of New York. Together we took many trips to the public library and Thomas carefully selected books filled with facts about New York State. He had several weeks to compile the information and many weekends were spent on worksheets to prepare for the final draft. Finally he had all the materials that were required and it was time to actually write his report. His assignment called for specific information. As we sat down together, I asked him to review the books he'd borrowed from the library. He did this. Then I reminded him of the criteria he was to follow according to the assignment. He said he understood. After I was sure he'd reviewed the material, I asked him to 'rephrase' the information. We started with one paragraph at a time. While working through several paragraphs, he suddenly stopped, turned to me and said, 'You know, Mom, I can't understand why I need to rephrase any of this information for my report.'

Before I could comment he blurted out, 'I think that this information is perfectly legible,' pointing to a paragraph from his library book.

Smiling, I said, 'You're right. It is legible. But that's not the point. You see, these books [I pointed to the stack of library books] on New York are to be used as a reference or a guide. The best part about writing a report is deciding what information you think is important, and putting it in your own words. That is what makes it your work. If you just retyped what someone else already wrote, that's just copying someone else's work. Do you understand what I mean?'

Thomas thought about what I told him and then said, 'I guess I understand. But, if I wrote something really good, like a sequel to the Yu-Gi-Oh movie or something, I wouldn't mind at all if someone used my exact script.'

'Why is that?'

'Because I think I'm a good writer. In fact, I wouldn't want anyone to change one word,' he said proudly.

Note: He missed the point, but it's nice to know he's a confident writer.

Winter break

Over winter break Thomas and I went to Southern California to visit friends. Around the sixth day of our vacation, Thomas started feeling homesick. As we walked on the beach together that afternoon, I noticed that he seemed particularly weepy. While trying to distract him for the remainder of the trek back, I decided to tell him a story. I invented a story about a stick that I had found and picked up on our beach walk. Thomas quickly named the stick Plank.

I carried Plank with us while we walked. Plank was relatively tan, slim and the size of a standard ruler. He was made of bamboo and seemed especially sturdy. Plank's age was a mystery, but based on his outward appearance we determined his age to be approximately four years old. His exterior was rough, clearly a result of the damp conditions he had suffered while existing on the beach. After careful study, we decided Plank looked tattered, tired and even gloomy.

I continued telling the story about how Plank had lived on the beach but seemed to be rather lonely. I explained that although it appeared that Plank had a life of freedom, as many children enjoyed playing with him and lots of dogs would run to fetch him, no one ever seemed to want to take him home. As a result, he was continuously left abandoned (probably heartbroken) on the beach. At this point in my story I glanced over at Thomas who was walking alongside of me, his head down, face red and eyes welling up with tears.

'What's wrong?' I asked him while patting his back.

'Nothing. Go on, Mom. What happened next?' he asked with a low shaken voice.

By Thomas' reaction, it was apparent to me that I needed to change the direction of the story and so I continued. 'One day, a little boy came upon Plank, who was quietly lying on his side in the sand. There were no other sticks around him. He was alone. The boy immediately noticed Plank, picked him up and used him to write his name in the sand. Then he used Plank's sharp tip and drew a detailed picture of a dinosaur in the sand. The boy was talented and creative and absolutely loved to draw. He and Plank drew and drew until it was time for the boy to go home.

'The boy thought of so many things he could do with Plank. Without thinking, he quickly planted Plank in his back pant pocket and took him home. Plank was eager to finally be with a boy who wanted him. At home, without hesitation, the boy determined that Plank needed to have a cheerful face. He held Plank, and with a blue and red marker, he drew two blue happy eyes and a big red smile. Plank's expression was joyful and the boy seemed pleased.'

At this point Thomas and I were almost to the hotel and so I was trying to wrap up the story. But again, as I glanced over to Thomas, I noticed he was still quite tearful.

'What's wrong?' I asked him. I thought the story had a nice finish and I couldn't understand what could have been so upsetting to him.

'Your story was so touching, Mom,' he said through tears as he wiped his eyes.

'Yeah, everyone was happy at the end, didn't you think?' I asked.

'I suppose. [Still crying] Mom, I want to take Plank home with me, okay?' he said. He was convinced that he had bonded with the stick that I was still holding. Then he informed me that he would be painting a face on him as soon as we returned to the hotel.

Given the circumstances and the clear possibility of a full blown emotional meltdown, I chose not to tell him that I was certain the airline wouldn't understand the bond between he and Plank, and unfortunately the stick would have to make other arrangements to get to our home.

There's more...

The next day, we arrived at the airport early to prepare for our flight home. After checking in, Thomas and I stood in the baggage claim line for only ten minutes before both of us were unexpectedly whisked off to the side. We were abruptly taken to a separate area, where two airport personnel informed me that they'd be examining our baggage and us. Startled, I asked why. They insisted it was routine procedure. Noticing no other mother and son team being routinely frisked, I firmly asked for an explanation.

I candidly explained that my son had special needs and that I did not want him to become worried or upset. To my surprise, they respectfully acknowledged my concern and continued their search calmly, explaining every step to Thomas in advance. When I glanced over at Thomas, who seemed unalarmed by the delay, I saw our baggage being carefully inspected. Plank, I thought. I instantly turned to Thomas and whispered, 'You didn't sneak Plank into your bag, did you?'

'No, I thought you were going to pack him,' Thomas replied.

Whew, I thought. If a child and his mother seemed suspicious, I wondered what would have happened if a happy face stick were found.

A few minutes later Thomas asked, 'Mom, if you didn't pack Plank, how is he getting home?'

'Um, I mailed him,' I heard myself say, not wanting to risk a meltdown

Note: Later, I was told that our tickets were red-flagged because we purchased our arrival and departure tickets on different days.

Reservoir walk

Walking around a reservoir path for exercise was one of Thomas' least favorite things to do. In fact, he'd describe it as 'torturous'. From start to finish it was less than three miles. It was a popular place to walk and not far from our home. I'd explained to him the benefits of the walk. 'Exercise is good for your heart, body and mind, Thomas. And don't forget all the different dogs and dog owners we get to meet along the way.' Still he'd complain about the ache in his small legs and the strain on his lungs. So melodramatic!

On this particular walk, with only a short while to go, Thomas abruptly stopped and sat on the ground to rest. When I explained to him that we'd only one mile to go, he dramatically fell on to the grass and told me how he thought he would wait for a wheelchair to arrive to 'wheel' him the rest of the way around the reservoir. Usually when he said something ridiculous or that just doesn't seem likely, I'd point out the probability of it actually happening.

Interestingly, as soon as I finished with my speech about how silly it would be to wait for a wheelchair, a woman walking behind us pushing an empty wheelchair offered Thomas a lift. Unbelievable! Her husband had injured his back and had been slowly walking behind her. She brought the wheel chair for him, just in case. Thomas leapt at the invitation and she agreed to push him for a short ride. As soon as he approached the chair, the woman asked Thomas if he would hold her purse and sweater. 'Why do I have to hold them?' he said bluntly (I wanted to die).

'Well, because they were sitting in the wheelchair and now there's no place to put them,' the woman said to Thomas, smiling at me.

'Oh, well sure,' he said, and then placed both in his lap while she pushed him along.

A few minutes later, he thanked her for the ride and we finished the rest of the hike on foot. As we walked further, Thomas informed me that wishing for a wheel chair actually wasn't so silly after all. He also took that opportunity to accurately point out that I was not always right.

Note: On the next sunny day, we again made the hike around the reservoir. Not a wheelchair in sight, much to Thomas' surprise.

Another day, same hike, different conversation, same complaint

'Mom, I wish I were Godlike,' Thomas announced.

'You mean kind, forgiving and incredibly wise,' I said, wondering what spurred the comment. I thought it was a pretty abstract thought and totally out of the blue.

Thomas stopped walking, looked at me and said, 'Well, you know what they say – one man's galoshes is another person's potpourri,' demonstrating his wisdom.

'So why again do you want to be Godlike?' I asked chuckling, still impressed with his interest in the topic.

'I mean like a Greek God, you know, so someone would carry me around this reservoir in one of those flat boards with handles so I wouldn't have to walk. And someone else could carry an umbrella to protect me from the sun,' Thomas said smiling.

'Oh brother!' I said.

Eye examination

Every few years, the State of California offers an eye exam to students at the elementary grade level. This exam is facilitated through the public school district. On this day, Thomas' classmates gathered to prepare for the activity. When it was Thomas' turn, he was asked by the examiner to step up to the line and cover one eye. He did this. Then the examiner instructed him to focus on the eye chart. While pointing to the letter E, the examiner asked Thomas, 'What's the next letter?'

'F,' Thomas replied.

The examiner shook her head no. Then, she pointed to the letter C on the chart and said to Thomas, 'and after this one?'

'D,' Thomas answered.

There was a noticeable silence between them. Then, appearing agitated, the examiner again pointed to the chart. 'What about this one,' she asked again, while pointing to the letter Z.

Thomas looked puzzled. 'I don't know,' he said. After a pause, 'A again?'

The examiner said nothing and looked at Thomas' fifth grade teacher, who'd been listening to their entire exchange. Quietly, she walked over to Thomas, pointed to the letter E on the chart and asked, 'Thomas, what is this letter?'

Through squinted eyes and alternating blinks, Thomas finally answered, 'Is it F?'

It was at that point that Thomas' teacher (not sure about the examiner) realized that he may in fact have difficulty seeing from a distance. It had never occurred to her before, as Thomas sat in the front of her class. He'd never complained about not being able to see her lessons on the board.

Based on that incident, I took Thomas to a friend of mine who is an optometrist to have him tested further. She was used to working with children on the Autistic spectrum. By the time the exam was finished, Thomas could name every machine used to identify his problem. The results indicated that he was near sighted and would require glasses. I was unsure about how he would feel about this news. To my surprise, Thomas was thrilled to know he would be able to choose a pair of glasses. He selected, of course, a cool pair of transitional lenses.

'They turn into sunglasses when I'm outside, Mom. Can you believe it? How cool is that?' He was thrilled. I was relieved.

Camp Loma Mar

In fifth grade, Thomas spent four days participating in outdoor education with his entire class. This was an adventure for him as well as for me. The week before Thanksgiving, three fifth grade classes from his elementary school, including Thomas' educational aide and principal, went to Camp Loma Mar. It was an old campground with rustic cabins nestled in the California Santa Cruz Mountains. He described his experience as 'memorable'. Although his cabin-mate was actually his educational aide, Mrs Trent, he spent most of the daylight hours hiking and exploring with his cabin-group. When asked about his favorite hike, Thomas described a beautiful forest hike. He explained that he enjoyed the card hike where the naturalist put down a collection of cards on a path for him and the others to follow. Some cards had arrows that pointed the way while other cards had information about the environment. However, the last card asked for the hiker to make a wish for the Earth.

Thomas read the card aloud and then took some time to consider his wish. The instructions on the card said to lie on the ground facing the sky, and to close his eyes while he made his wish. He did this. Several moments later, Thomas turned to Mrs Trent, who was also lying on the ground facing the sky, and said, 'My wish is that the Earth will be able to defend itself against the growing human population.' Mrs Trent was stunned. She just looked intently at Thomas, amazed by the maturity of his response.

Later when she recounted the story, she commented to me about his depth and insight. She told me that he didn't ask her about her wish (luckily), as her wish was that earth would help her make it down the hill without falling! She was pleased to share that story with me and other teachers, as another example of Thomas' genuine concern for the Earth and of course his literal mind.

Misunderstanding

'I can't wait to see the special effects show, Mom,' Thomas announced with absolute excitement in his voice. Although it was his second trip to Universal Studios, it was his first visit since deciding he wanted to become a famous filmmaker. His interest in the film industry ignited after researching writer and director George Lucas for a class report. Being a Star Wars fan, Thomas' aspirations further expanded, making 'film production' his new life's ambition.

Thomas and I sat in the audience watching a stage of 'actors' produce in sequence the phases of visual and audio special effects. They described in detail how images and sounds were incorporated into film, giving the illusion of reality. And they were convincing. So much so, that at the end of the final act, Thomas was horrified to realise that one of the actors had disappeared, never to be seen again (although it was clearly implied to the audience that it was part of the act). As the audience left the area, Thomas stayed back and asked to talk to one of the other actors on the set. I stood quietly beside him.

'Excuse me, sir, but what happened to the man that disappeared?' Thomas asked, concerned. He was very emotional and the actor immediately called the missing actor over to Thomas. Although Thomas was relieved, he firmly questioned the missing actor, 'So why did you lie?'

'Oh, it was a joke. A trick, you know an illusion. Were you upset?' the actor asked sincerely.

'Yes. And, actually, I think you lied. You shouldn't pretend you're dead if you're not. It's not nice,' Thomas said and walked away.

Later in the day, Thomas asked to see the show again. We did. Because he knew exactly what to expect, he found that show to be hysterically funny. 'I guess it was a joke,' he told me.

Note: In the next show I noticed that the missing actor reappeared at the end of the performance. Interesting!

Chapter Eight

Thomas-isms

Thomas has a unique way of expressing himself. He seems to collect words and string them together in context appropriately, with a sense of humor. I call them, Thomas-isMs

***

The day before Thomas' principal was to be transferred to another school, seemingly bothered by the change of events, he walked into her office and announced, 'Why the heck would anyone want to move to Arizona anyway? Don't you know it's hot there?' She smiled, knowing the change might be hard for him. Later, he told a friend, 'California just won't be the same without Mrs Garton.' When his friend tried to reassure him that it would; Thomas responded, 'No, I mean that literally. There will be one less person in California.'

***

After a particularly long day, I found myself having to repeat myself to Thomas. I was either asking him to tidy his room, complete his homework or finish his dinner, when out of sheer frustration he turned to me and said,

'You are so harsh. I hate the fact that I'm a minor.'

***

'Mom, unfortunately something's wrong with the copier,' Thomas announced in a panic.

'Something like what?' I wanted to know. It was a brand new copier.

'Well, the words 'paper jam – paper jam', keeps blinking.' (Long pause)

'Actually, it should say 'foil jam – foil jam'. I was experimenting,'
he confessed.

***

Following a difficult day at school involving math, one of Thomas' teachers tried to explain to him how necessary math was in daily routines and how it was used in almost every profession. Thinking about it for a while, he later told his teacher, 'You know, I've been thinking, I could become a comedian. I think that's a job that doesn't require any math.'

During the earlier years in elementary school, Thomas was known by the school staff as being extremely sensitive to loud noises. He often had to wear ear plugs just to attend school assemblies or music class. Once, during his later years there, he attended a school musical and noticed a little girl next to him sitting in her teacher's lap and covering her ears. Thomas leaned over to the teacher and whispered, 'What's wrong with her? Why is she covering her ears?' Being quite familiar with Thomas' own sensitivity to noise, the teacher thought Thomas would be able to identify with her aversion to 'noise' and answered back, 'She's kind of sensitive to sound.'

'Wow, that's kind of strange!' Thomas replied, appearing utterly surprised. The teacher was amused by his response and thought it was interesting that he couldn't see himself in that girl.

'Well, why doesn't she use ear plugs?' he offered.

* * *

One morning before school, Thomas woke up late and was having to rush to get ready. He said he was tired and was complaining about having to get up so early.

'Why do I have to go to school anyway?' he asked, feeling rushed to eat his breakfast.

'I know, it's a pain sometimes,' I said in agreement.

'That wasn't a rhetorical question, Mom,' he said, shaking his head.

'Why do I have to go to school?' he asked again.

* * *

We arrived at the school one morning and walked toward his classroom when I turned to him and asked, 'So how is Mrs Trent (his educational aide) doing?'

'I have no idea. I haven't seen her yet this morning,' he told me.

* * *

While on a walk one day, Thomas became tired (and theatrical) and said he was thirsty. He started yelling, 'Waaatteeeerrr…[clutching his throat with his hands and taking large slow steps] I need waaateeerrr…'

'Thomas, if you're thirsty, just say so,' I told him.

'Okay. Mom, I need H2O in a liquid state,' he said plainly.

* * *

One Sunday I spent the entire day in the bathroom sick from the 'flu. Thomas walked in at one point and said to me, 'Mom, you should take a sick day today.' Before I could say anything in response he walked away shouting, 'You're not contagious or anything, are you Mom?'

* * *

Thomas was walking back from lunch recess with Mrs Trent where he'd been pretending to be a swami. With his sweatshirt wrapped high around his head as if he were wearing a turban he said, 'I'm going to predict your future.'

Mrs Trent replied, 'Okay, as long as I receive lots of money and get to go to Hawaii on vacation.'

Thomas paused and then said with a voice of authority, 'Okay, but you're to donate half of your money to a lovable boy named Thomas, whom you once knew.'

Mrs Trent laughed and asked, 'Okay, but do I still get to go to Hawaii?'

'Of course!' he assured her.

* * *

During a speech session at school, Thomas was asked by his speech teacher, 'So who do you play with at recess?'

'My imagination. What do you think?' He informed her.

'Who do you think you should play with at recess?' she inquired.

'Anyone that understands me; but that's nobody but you adults and you don't have time for me,' he said bluntly.

* * *

Thomas was taking a math test and Mrs Trent was sitting next to him. She was checking one of his answers and thought he'd mixed up two of the probleMs She leaned over him and told him to check the problems again, but then realised she'd actually mixed up the problems, not Thomas. 'Never mind,' she told him. 'You know what you're doing. Don't listen to me.'

Without glancing up he said, 'Sometimes I wonder how you got hired.'

'I was hired because I told the school district that I wanted to be inspired by a 'brilliant child' and they said we have just the student. His name is Thomas,' she said warmly.

'Oh,' Thomas said, as if it made perfect sense to him.

* * *

I poked my head into Thomas' bedroom to see if he was sleeping yet and said, 'I know you're still awake. I saw you smile.'

'Betrayed by my own emotion,' Thomas quipped.

***

While studying for a quiz, Thomas was explaining to me the definition of matter. I remembered being impressed with his knowledge and commented, 'You are so smart, Thomas.'

'Yes I know, but sometimes I think it's a disadvantage.'

'How so?' I asked.

'If you're the smartest kid in the group, sometimes it's more of a liability. You know, the responsibility of always being right!' he told me.

Chapter Nine

Advocacy

When you become a parent you wear many hats. However, a hat labeled 'advocate' is one you probably didn't expect to wear. That is until you realise that your child had special needs that require special services. For a child who has encyclopedic knowledge but whom is socially challenged, the problem is often difficult to understand, let alone diagnose or address. But once a diagnosis has been established a plan can be developed. Eventually, you will discover how and when to advocate for your child.

About me as a parent and an advocate…

I am a huge believer in having more than one plan. I figured out a long time ago that good coping strategies were a necessity of life, especially in college. I always had several plans in place, alleviating the potential anxiety from an unanticipated situation.

For example, once, back in college, I remember taking an Epidemiology course and needed at least a B on the blue book exam to make the grade I wanted. I studied very hard and was confident I would receive an adequate grade on the test. On the day of the exam, when the blue books were passed out, I noticed that much of the information I'd studied so diligently was not on the exam. In reviewing the test questions, I honestly believed that they were not representative of the course material or lectures presented in class. Instead of getting freaked out, I quickly came up with plan B. I wrote a note to my professor explaining why I was re-writing a number of his test questions. I expanded on what I thought more accurately reflected the course material. After clearly stating my position, I answered each one of my questions honestly and completely. Given the circumstances, I felt I had no other choice.

To my surprise, my professor graded my work and announced to the class, without pointing me out, that if in the future a student felt the need to challenge the course material on an exam, he would consider their input. I received a B on that blue book test.

My point is simple. Developing a plan is a coping skill that I've used, and it's proved to be effective for me. I have conditioned myself to have an A, B and C plan when it comes to advocating for Thomas. A plan may include borrowing parts of a program, adding strategies, and incorporating essential services that are unique to Thomas' needs and how he learns. In terms of coping techniques, adopting multiple plans with flexibility has been important for Thomas to learn, in response to the unexpected situations that occur in his every day life.

I found that I didn't quite understand how Thomas thought or communicated in the earlier years, I educated myself about Autistic Spectrum Disorders and later Asperger's syndrome. In doing so, I researched using the internet, read books, attended conferences and spoke to professionals in the field about ASD. I learned what support services were available and accessed them. Then I created a plan. Wanting the best for him, I was motivated to share with his teachers as much as I knew about how Thomas processed information. This was well received. My idea was that if I could help him build a solid foundation where he could find success in the classroom, he would progress and move forward.

In speaking with many parents over the years, I've discovered that many children with an ASD diagnosis weren't always identified until they entered elementary school. This, I have found, is when the disparity is most obvious. I too was under the assumption that the school district would know exactly what to do for Thomas in terms of special education and support services. I was wrong. I realised rather quickly that the school district and I had different perspectives. Specifically, our differences were between what was considered to be appropriate versus necessary. As a result, conflict ensued.

Why?

There are a number of reasons why. Lack of knowledge and understanding about Autism Spectrum Disorders, unavailable or unqualified service providers and budget limitations were several of the underlying issues that perpetuated the friction. Inconsistency and the lack of agreement regarding what is 'most appropriate' further complicated the problem.

What did you do? What can I do?

I educated myself on the rights and responsibilities of my child. Parents can learn about the Individuals with Disabilities Education Act (IDEA), the American Disability Act (ADA) and a Free and Appropriate Public Education (FAPE). Find out about the special education program in your district and the services they offer. Research the sequence of events in terms of assessments and diagnosis. Understand the Local Education Agency (LEA) and the programs they have available. Research as many programs as possible and decide which ones meet the needs of your child.

What is an IEP?

An IEP is an Individual Educational Program. A child with special needs fitting certain criteria is offered an IEP because they require a specific educational program. A meeting occurs between the parents of the special needs child and members of the school district. The purpose is to come to an agreement, outlining a specific program in which your child will be appropriately educated according to their unique needs under the law. Sometimes this is a 'special' day classroom environment with fewer students and special educators, and sometimes this means a general education setting (fully inclusive) with neurotypical peers and support services. Services are decided upon in the IEP meeting, following assessments indicating a need. These may include: pragmatic speech and language, occupational therapy, behavioral therapy, resource assistance, adapted physical education, social skills program and a one-on-one aide. Once the IEP team agrees on the appropriate services for the child, an IEP agreement is signed by the team and services begin.

Note: The parent is an equal part of the IEP team.

Creating programs

What did you do? What can I do?

At times, Thomas' concentration on his special interests became such an issue for him that it often excluded the opportunity for peer social interaction. When he was in second grade, I thought he would benefit from a social skills 'lunch-bunch' group involving neurotypical peers. The IEP team agreed and a weekly interactive group activity was written into his IEP agreement and facilitated by his SLP, Aide and RS. A permission slip was created and sent home to the parents of the general education students. Fortunately the idea was well received and the 'lunch-bunch' was quite successful. This was offered through fifth grade.

Note: by fourth and fifth grade – the 'lunch-bunch' is known as the 'Cartooning Club'.

Dear 2nd Grade Families,

The lunch-bunch is now happening every Thursday at lunch recess. It's a time when a small group of children get together to share lunch and play games. Indoor and outdoor activities including cartooning, board games, art projects and sport activities will be available. An adult will facilitate this program and each week will be a new and exciting activity.

The goal is to provide and encourage an environment that will enhance your child's social skill development in a small group setting. The lunch-bunch sign up sheet will be available on my classroom door every Monday.

If your child would like to participate in this program, please return this signed permission slip.

Sincerely,

Your teacher

What is an In-service Day?

Based on Thomas' unpleasant kindergarten experience, I requested that an in-service day about Autism Spectrum Disorders, specifically Asperger's syndrome, be written into his IEP agreement. As most of the teachers and staff at Thomas' elementary school were not familiar with Autism Spectrum Disorders at the time, the in-service day gave them an opportunity to discuss learning differences and processing issues often found with children on the autism spectrum.

As it was the first in-service of its kind, a program specialist from the school district, with educational training in autism, provided the staff with literature about autism spectrum disorder's. In addition, I spoke about Asperger's syndrome and Thomas, sharing stories that illustrated how he thought and interpreted information. Later a video was shown demonstrating how children who were along the autism spectrum learned in a typical school setting. The entire school staff attended, ending with a constructive question and answer period. It was extremely productive, and set a precedent for the following year.

I've learned so much from my son over the years. For instance, practical and purposeful communication is something he understands and relies on, while casual or social conversation is extremely difficult for him to interpret. He requires consistency and continuity to maintain focus, but recognises that the interpretation and actual meaning of language are often different. These are skills he slowly continues to acquire over time and with practice. Thomas received five years of pragmatic speech from different speech therapists. Many of his goals and objectives were developed following the philosophy and strategies created by Michelle Garcia Winner, an SLP and founder of her Centre for Social Thinking.

What are Support Services?

They are services that support the student in their areas of need. According to IDEA, every child is entitled to a Free and Appropriate Public Education in the least restrictive environment. Therefore, based on the needs of each student, every public school district has the responsibility of providing the necessary services for a Special Education student, as they would to every other student.

Thomas was able to be fully included in a general education setting with the support of a one-on-one educational aide. Essentially her role was to monitor his overall educational instruction and assist in the interpretation of academic lessons for him. Sometimes that meant restating questions or directions to be more specific. Occasionally it meant reviewing an assignment or previewing a test – with modifying or accommodations as needed.

Academically

In the earlier years of elementary school, the role of Thomas' aide was primarily to keep him involved and on task with the rest of the class. Although Thomas was advanced in a number of academic areas, clearly capable of grade level work with the exception of math, he nevertheless required the assistance of his aide. In a nutshell, she assumed the responsibility of being the 'glue' between him and all of his other services providers. Other helpful support services included Pragmatic Speech and Language Therapy addressing pragmatic language and social skills, Occupational Therapy to address fine and gross motor issues, Behavioral Consultation creating a positive behavior plan, Resource Assistance to address academic deficits, and a peer social skills group a lunch-bunch program with neurotypical peers to practice social interaction.

Socially

Thomas' aide actively assisted him in becoming more engaged with his peers. As his preference was to isolate himself from others, she would prompt him using scripted language and Social Stories to initiate peer interaction. This was often modeled or rehearsed before entering unstructured settings such as recess and at lunch period.

Several methods of positive reinforcement were used regularly to motivate appropriate behavior and to promote independence. For example, a daily responsibility sheet was used as a visual guide to measure independent growth and academic progress. For Thomas, earning computer minutes was his motivator. Free computer time was important to him, proving to be effective. In addition, Thomas' aide kept a daily communication log that detailed his school day. This was reviewed by the classroom teacher and was sent home at the end of each day. The communication log was extremely helpful because it provided me with the opportunity to talk to him about his school day, which was otherwise difficult for him to recount.

Thomas' IEP agreement periodically included a behaviorist who developed a behavior plan specific to Thomas' needs and altered when necessary. It was implemented by all of his service providers at school and was fundamentally important for his program to be effective. His behaviorist was amazing.

Final note

It's important to note that currently in the United States, the criteria in the Diagnostic & Statistical Manual (Fourth Edition) referencing Asperger's syndrome, is often used by professionals in determining an autistic spectrum diagnosis. And although it's been stated in the past that one distinguishing characteristic of AS is the absence of significant language delay, more recently it has been thought that some children with early language delays have been later diagnosed with Asperger's syndrome. The DSM-IV Text Revision offers a broader and more complete definition.

What I have learned through this process

As your child changes developmentally and cognitively, so must the intervention, education and advocacy.

Chapter Ten

Final Thoughts

Thomas is aware that he's been diagnosed with Asperger's syndrome and he realises that he sometimes perceives the world differently. When discussed, I describe Asperger's to him as being 'just a word', not a definition. I do, however, explain it as part of the reason why his perception of people and situations are often unlike others. I've explained that his way of thinking is distinctive, much like the way he processes information.

Whenever possible, I extend our discussions to emphasize his wonderful strengths and amazing skills. I remind him of his nearly photographic memory and his remarkable artistic talent. I point out his ability to be creative and I marvel at his amazing imagination.

I often highlight his intelligence, while drawing attention to his insight on the subject of science. He's always been an advanced reader with great comprehension. His precise and extensive knowledge in his chosen areas of interest are astounding. But mostly, I tell him how proud I am of his kind heart and gentle spirit. And although I believe him to be charming, loving and unbelievably funny, what he believes about himself is fundamentally important. Over the years I think Thomas has grown to appreciate his own talents and remarkable skills. He recognises them as gifts, and so do I. Thomas is living his best life!

Epilogue

Dear Mom,

This elementary school is pretty cool. I wonder what middle school will be like. Here are my favorite things to do: Do some artwork because I'm the next Van Gough, do science because I have Asperger's syndrome, and complaining about Math because, okay – there's no reason.

Here are some things I'm most proud of:

Outdoor Ed because I got to pretend I was a predator, the computer so I can write screenplays, and the fact that AFX* got a new member.

I think I've improved the most in my independence because I do things independently, like typing this letter. Here are my goals for middle school and beyond:

To make movies, study dinosaurs and to take over the world.

Mha, ha, ha, ha (just kidding about the last part).

Your son,

TJB

*Alpha Force Extreme

Appendix

Abbreviations and acronyms used in this book:

AB	Assembly Bill for California
ADA	American Disabilities Act
AS	Asperger's syndrome
ASD	Autism Spectrum Disorder
AT	Assistive Technology
CAC	Community Advisory Committee
CASE	Community Alliance for Special Education
DSM IV	Diagnostic and Statistical Manual of the American Psychiatric Association
FAPE	Free Appropriate Public Education
GFCF	Gluten Free & Casein Free
IDEA	Individuals with Disabilities Education Act
IEP	Individualised Education Program
IQ	Intelligence Quotient
LEA	Local Education Agency
LRE	Least Restrictive Environment
NLD	Non-Verbal Learning Disorder
OT	Occupational Therapy
PCP	Primary Care Physician
PDD	Pervasive Developmental Disorder
PT	Physical Therapy
PAI	Protection and Advocacy Incorporated
RCEB	Regional Center of the East Bay

RS	Resource Specialist
SB	Senate Bill
SELPA	Special Education Local Plan Area
SH	Severely Handicapped
SID	Sensory Integration Dysfunction
SLP	Speech and Language Pathologist

References

Karra Barber
Autistic Spectrum Resources
www.aspergersresource.org

Tony Attwood, PhD
www.tonyattwood.com.au/

Michelle Winner's Center for Social Thinking Pragmatic Language and
Social Skills
Michelle Garcia Winner, SLP
www.socialthinking.com

The Gray Center for Social Learning & Understanding
Gray,C.(2001) *My Social Stories Book*. London: Jessica Kingsley Publishers
www.thegraycenter.org

David Berg, Educational Therapist
www.makingmathreal.org

Jeanette McAfee, M.D.
www.jeaniemcafee.com

Gluten Free Casein Free Diet
www.GFCFDiet.com

Sensory Integration Therapy
www.out-of-sync-child.com

American Occupational Therapy Association
www.aota.org

Council for Exceptional Children
www.ideapractices.org

Circle of Friends
Forest, M. & Pearpoint, J. (1992) *Commonsense Tools: Maps and Circles*.
Inclusion Papers. Toronto: Inclusion Press

Forest, M. (1992) *Inclusion Papers*. Toronto: Inclusion Press

Maines, B. & Robinson, G. (1998) *All For Alex - A Circle of Friends*. Bristol:
Lucky Duck Publishing.

MORE ASPERGER'S SYNDROME TITLES

Social Skills and Austistic Spectrum Disorders

Lynn Plimley, **Maggie Bowen** and **Hugh Morgan**

This book examines the concerns around inappropriate social behaviour that those living and working with children and adults with ASDs face on a day-to-day basis.

Autistic Spectrum Disorder Support Kit
A Paul Chapman Publishing title
2006 • 96 pages
Hardback (1-4129-2312-3) / Paperback (1-4129-2313-1)

Autistic Spectrum Disorders in the Early Years

Lynn Plimley, **Maggie Bowen** and **Hugh Morgan**

Looking at the early years of a child's life, this book provides information on the services that are available for those from birth to five years, and addresses issues related to identification, assessment, teaching and learning and family support.

Autistic Spectrum Disorder Support Kit
A Paul Chapman Publishing title
2006 • 96 pages
Hardback (1-4129-2314-X) / Paperback (1-4129-2315-8)

Living with Autistic Spectrum Disorders
Guidance for Parents, Carers and Siblings

Elizabeth Attfield and **Hugh Morgan**

By giving a concise account of what life may be like following the diagnosis of ASDs in the family, this book examines service provision at different stages, and provides information for parents, carers and practitioners.

Autistic Spectrum Disorder Support Kit
A Paul Chapman Publishing title
2006 • 96 pages
Hardback (1-4129-2328-X) / Paperback (1-4129-2329-8)

Autistic Spectrum Disorders in the Secondary School

Lynn Plimley and **Maggie Bowen**

This book looks at all of the new factors which must be considered when young people with ASDs make the transition from primary to secondary school.

Autistic Spectrum Disorder Support Kit
A Paul Chapman Publishing title
2006 • 96 pages
Hardback (1-4129-2310-7) / Paperback (1-4129-2311-5)

Supporting Pupils with Autistic Spectrum Disorders
A Guide for School Support Staff

Lynn Plimley and **Maggie Bowen**

This provides information and professional guidance for people working in educational support with pupils from across the autistic spectrum.

Autistic Spectrum Disorder Support Kit
A Paul Chapman Publishing title
2006 • 96 pages
Hardback (1-4129-2316-6) / Paperback (1-4129-2317-4)

Helping Pupils with Autistic Spectrum Disorders to Learn

Mary Pittman *University of Plymouth*

This book looks at how to help pupils understand the concept of change in their daily routines, so that this understanding has a positive effect on their behaviour and ability to access the curriculum.

A Paul Chapman Publishing title
2006 • 144 pages
Hardback (1-4129-1965-7) / Paperback (1-4129-1966-5)

Educating Pupils with Autistic Spectrum Disorders
A Practical Guide

Martin Hanbury *Landgate School, Wigan*

'Martin Hanbury is full of enthusiasm and is extremely knowledgeable' - *Cathy Mercer, National Autistic Society*

This book will help practitioners to employ appropriate teaching and learning strategies when working with those in their classroom who experience an ASD.

A Paul Chapman Publishing title
2005 • 144 pages
Hardback (1-4129-0227-4) / Paperback (1-4129-0228-2)

Martian in the Playground
Understanding the Schoolchild with Asperger's Syndrome

Clare Sainsbury

WINNER OF TES/NASEN BEST ACADEMIC BOOK AWARD 2000

'This book will be if interest to all who are involved with Asperger's Syndrome: parents, professionals and the young people themselves'
- *Dr Jane Shields, Director NAS Earlybird Centre*

Lucky Duck Books
2000 • 140 pages
Paperback (1-87394-208-7)

Paul Chapman Publishing
A SAGE Publications Company

Lucky Duck Books

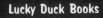

MORE ASPERGER'S SYNDROME TITLES

The Asperger Love Guide

A Practical Guide for Adults with Asperger's Syndrome to Seeking, Establishing and Maintaining Successful Relationships

Genevieve Edmonds and **Dean Worton**

'The National Autistic Society find this a helpful guide' - *Cathy Mercer, NAS*

Here, Genevieve and Dean, both adults with Asperger's Syndrome, share their advice and tips for romantic success.

Lucky Duck Books
2005 • 92 pages
Hardback (1-4129-2324-7) / Paperback (1-4129-1910-X)

The Asperger Social Guide

How to Relate to Anyone in any Social Situation as an Adult with Asperger's Syndrome

Genevieve Edmonds and **Dean Worton**

'Social skills are a big problem area for people with AS, so quality help is always needed' - *Cathy Mercer, NAS*

This book is a self-help manual written by two AS adults who offer others the benefits of their experiences.

Lucky Duck Books
2006 • 120 pages
Hardback (1-4129-2023-X) / Paperback (1-4129-2024-8)

The Asperger Personal Guide

Raising Self-Esteem and Making the Most of Yourself as a Adult with Asperger's Syndrome

Genevieve Edmonds and **Dean Worton**

Lucky Duck Books
2006 • 150 pages
Paperback (1-4129-2257-7)

Glass Half-Empty, Glass Half-Full

How Asperger's Syndrome Changed My Life

Chris Mitchell

This gripping and at times astonishing story will be inspirational to all adults either facing Asperger's Syndrome personally or interacting with someone who has been diagnosed

Lucky Duck Books
2005 • 104 pages
Hardback (1-4129-2047-7) • / Paperback (1-4129-1162-1)

Children Can Learn With Their Shoes Off

Supporting Students with Asperger's Syndrome in Mainstream Schools and Colleges

A4 Book and Video

Barbara Maines

This extensive resource features the excellent, flexible and imaginative ways in which adults working in schools can improve the learning and social experience for students with ASDs.

Lucky Duck Books
2002 • 36 pages
Video (1-87394-289-3) / Paperback (1-4129-2033-7)

Aspects of Asperger's

Success in the Teens and Twenties

Maude Brown and **Alex Miller**

A thought provoking and practical book about how one supporter, a grandmother, helped her granddaughter search for ways to help her overcome the difficulties they both faced.

Lucky Duck Books
2004 • 82 pages
Paperback (1-904315-12-7)

Standing Down Falling Up

Asperger's Syndrome from the Inside Out

Nita Jackson

'This book is easy to read and one to recommend to colleagues, parents and possibly some young people with Asperger's Syndrome' - *Support of Learning*

This book is a fascinating account of Nita Jackson's experience of Aspergers Syndrome.

Lucky Duck Books
2002 • 134 pages
Paperback (1-87394-298-2)

From Another Planet

Autism from Within

Dominique Dumortier

'This is one of those books that someone could pick up and read and could open the door to recognition of a condition that has so far been undetected' - *Stroud Autistic Support Group*

Lucky Duck Books
2004 • 112 pages
Paperback (1-904315-32-1) • £12.99

Visit our website at **www.paulchapmanpublishing.co.uk** for more Autism and Asperger's Syndrome titles

 **Paul Chapman Publishing**
A SAGE Publications Company

Lucky Duck Books

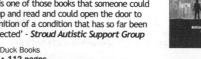